AF400000

Maher Asaad Baker

Lullabies of Time

ISBN Softcover: 978-3-384-45964-0

ISBN Hardback: 978-3-384-45965-7

ISBN E-Book: 978-3-384-45966-4

Cover image designed by Freepik

Contents

Introduction

France is a country located mainly in the heart of Europe. The culture and folklore of France its many inheritances are the music and folklore of France, which are testaments of the unity of the country's rich heritage, which changed during the centuries. When initiating a journey into French music and folklore, one is walking through a historical landscape populated by tradition and invention, regional distinctions and the pervasive effect of history.

The earl of medieval French music was at once in the time when the oral tradition of folk music was a lifeblood in communities. It was the troubadours and trouvères, poet musicians from the south and North of France respectively that echoed through the courts and castles of the land. Intricate tapestries of love, chivalry and social commentary, their songs were often d with the accompaniment of the lute, vielle (a medieval fiddle) and flute accompanied. Rooted in folk tradition, but on this evidence, the influence of the Catholic Church's liturgical music — its solemn, its polyphony — was evident in this music as well. Medieval French music was characterized by an interactivity of the sacred and secular elements which reflects the dependency of the Church and the Nobility, two major influences on the country's cultural environment of the period.

The medieval era is where our French music story starts as French music was the oral tradition of folk music that kept communities alive. From the court and castles of 'the land,' the music of the troubadours and trouvères, poet-musician troubadours and north of France respectively, resounded. Introspective and intricate tapestries of love, chivalry, and social commentary, very often accompanied by the lute, vielle (a medieval fiddle) and flute, their songs were performed. This was rooted in folk tradition, but, like the folk music of its day, was marked by the influence of the liturgical music of the Catholic Church, with solemn chants and polyphonic compositions thereof. Medieval French music's blending of the sacred and secular corresponded to the proximity, symbiosis of, and rivalry between the Church and the nobility, two institutional powers among the milieu of authoritative forces imbricated in the cultural history of the era.

France was at the crossroads of Renaissance artistic and intellectual revival at the dawn of the Renaissance. This period was marked by an exploding interest in humanism, the philosophy that man, not God, was the centre of the universe. The secularization of music was echoed in an increase of composers' themes such as the earth, love, and the human experience. While composers like Josquin des Prez and Clément Janequin fashioned chansons which were both musically complex and deeply expressive, looking like picture books, they seem to have strived to tell the story of their age through their vivid portraiture of everyday life.

At the same time, the folk music of France proceeded, as did the disparate cultures inherited from the myriad tradings crossing the

Mediterranean in the centuries leading up to the 60s. Each region had its musical language, from the Celtic set to Brittany and Occitan in the south to the Spanish in the north. Variations in both the types of instruments and those who played them were great: bagpipes of central France, for example, hurdy-gurdy of the Auvergne and tambourine of Provence each added to the rich sonic tapestry of French folklore. Rather, the development of these regions in question contributed to, and were not isolated phenomena, on the broader fabric of French musical identities. They intercalated and encrusted with one another to breed a contriver and ordinarily developing musical scene.

The Baroque period was an era of sophistication and wealth, and in the ornate and tremendously detailed compositions which characterize the Baroque period. French Baroque music is the very example of music that is elegant, refined, and straight from classical harmony. Its musical language was identical to the music of Lully and Couperin. During Louis XIV – the Sun King – the court was a hub of musical innovation, with the king being such an important part of the artistic trends of this period. It was not simply music in Baroque, neither a means of entertainment, but a powerful means of propaganda in its time, to promote absolute monarchy, and the divine right of kings.

But as the French aristocracy revelled in the splendour of Baroque music, the folk traditions of France had impressed themselves on the common people. It was through the songs and dances of the peasantry that cultural heritage was preserved, communal values expressed and hardships of ordinary life survived. Folk traditions were not fixed though, but adapted and evolved for new social and economic needs. For instance during the time of the Industrial Revolution the rural landscape changed greatly causing people from the country to move to the cities. The process of urbanization had such an important effect on French folklore, as traditional songs and dances were transplanted to new environments and sweated out by experience of urban life.

The history of French music and folklore turned a corner with the French Revolution of 1789. For these revolutionary ideals of liberty, equality, and fraternity found expression in this music, new composers, such as Étienne Méhul and François-Joseph Gossec, composed works which celebrated the people's victory over tyranny. The revolution also rekindled a long repressed interest in folk music as the new republic attempted to establish a national identity based on the national traditions of the people.

Yet when France reached the 19th century the Romantic movement swept across Europe and had an indelible mark on French music. As the emotional intensity and expressive freedom of Romanticism so inspired Hector Berlioz and Charles Gounod, so their name was drawn upon to create works that explore the extremes of human passion, and the sublime grandeur of nature. As in Poland, too, the Romantic spirit shaped the folk music of France, which was collected by such people as Théodore Hersart de La Villemarqué and François-Marie Luzel, who preserved the songs and tales of the regions. Their efforts stoked the flames of larger efforts to revitalize France's own roots, a time in which the nation was seeking to reestablish its cultural heritage in the wake of high modernization.

Later in the 20th century French music and folklore were further changed. Deep scars on the cultural psyche of the nation remained from the two World Wars. As the interwar years witnessed a revival in interest in traditional French folk music, artists such as Georges Brassens and Édith Piaf drew on the abundant past of the chanson to create a new, more popular form on which to base their songwriting, that could speak to working-class experience.

After World War, though, France found itself in the middle of a wave of fast cultural and social change, brought about by global and technological changes reshaping the musical landscape. The advent of rock and roll, jazz, and all the international musical styles imposed a challenge on the dominance of traditional French music and eventually drew the styles together into new musical genres.

As a result, today the music and folklore of France still testify to the country's long historical history. Unlike much of the music of northern Europe, the story of French music is one of constant evolution and mutation, structured by the simultaneous interaction of tradition and innovation, the faithful reflection of past glories and the inescapable imprint of historical events, even when they are not yet in the past. Exploring this story, entering this world, is to almost arbitrarily immerse oneself in the cultural heart of France, to see the spirit of the people and the soul of the nation expressed in the most spontaneous and powerful way possible: through music.

Origins

In Palaeolithic times, well before the invention of writing, man created music and other forms of rituals as a cultural phenomenon. It has been established that prehistoric man had a variety of instruments in the form of horns, drums, rattles and flutes. Perhaps these instruments were used in singing and dancing ceremonies of solidarity, hunting, fertility, cursing, and healing, ceremonial and animistic prayers, ancestral communion, and other customs and creeds. In the course of thousands of millennia, Paleolithic and Neolithic peoples gradually evolved a higher type of musical and religious art.

The Celts, who filled ancient Gaul (that is to say most of what is now France) during the Bronze and Iron Ages, were necessarily part and parcel of the musical and oral traditions inherent in their societies. The prehistoric motivation of the Celtic artwork was in poetic song and PVC that narrated exotic stories of heroism and mythology. However, in the Celtic society bards and musicians were honored as dignified persons. Bards were the preservers of the cultural memory; they recited hundreds of heroic and lyrical songs and tunes, as well as numerous ballads, and handed them on to descendants. Music was related to the rituals of the solstice and agricultural feast. Paganism as seen in the Celtic religion incorporated gods, plants, most animals and the land, thus had a strong philosophical inclination.

Music played a significant role also in Celtic warfare. Shakking horns were blown loudly instructing the enemies they were unterable they had to surrender. Drums set cadence for marching music when warriors went to battle. War songs were songs of triumph and celebrated good fighters; lullabies were songs of sorrow and grief. Courtship and love were prominent motives in the bardic material; actual music included sonnets calling attention to the worthy qualities of the beloved gents and ladies. At feasts, and other public events where a recital was to be presented, bards were accompanied by large bells and lyres. It is believed that dancers depicted new staking cycles, initiation ceremonies, mythological themes, and any other traditions of that tribe.

To this context, interactions and sometimes clashes with the Romans grew during mediaeval period due to the expansion of

Celtic people into the Roman territories. Celts of Gaul were conquered by Rome in the second to fifth centuries CE and through the conversion of figures and motifs of the Roman / early Christian culture into Celtic styles, aspects of these civilizations melded together slowly. Writing as well as speaking of Latin was formally brought to the mainstream. Through roads, trade and cities the Gallic people were Romanised. Christianity gradually wrestled pagan backwaters. These drastic transformations occurred in the vaster Gallo-Roman context, even so, ancient folkways continued.

In the medieval period, the bards became known as classical poets, with a thorough acquaintance of the epic legend of the Celts and its heroes, Vercingetorix. They passed intact historical information on local plants and their use in medicine, traditional ways of grapevine cultivation for wine production, sacred groves associated with gods and spirits, springs which were regarded as divine sources etc. There were folk dances and music, costumes, and drama performed and still persisted, changing with the transforming social-cultural context under Roman imperial colonialization. Some elements of Celtic Gaulish culture, such as languages, bagpipes and fiddles and so on, and the celebration of feast, were maintained when the area was devastated in 407 or 408 CE and the Western Roman Empire formally collapsed in 476 CE.

By 6th century CE, the Merovingian Dynasty has also made its foothold over Frankish over the region. Even so, marks left by the Celtic and the Gallo-Roman presence were hardcarved and impossible to erase. Performers of old, however, had recorded pagan supernatural beliefs and agricultural praxis in folk and oral narratives and later in manuscript and printed ballads, lyric poetry, romance, illuminated manuscripts, choral and other liturgical music, and early drama or mystery play fragments. For several millennia of prehistoric and early medieval creation on Gallic territory, musicians and visionary artists imbued the culture with the legacy that eventually led to a uniquely French style.

Musical Instruments of France have a long history with the many traditional musical instruments of France which can be dated back to the ancient or medieval period. Musical instruments such as the hurdy-gurdy, bagpipes, vielle and flutes were well known household and travelling instruments among peasants and travellers in the countryside of France for many centuries and were used for the purpose of utility and enjoyment. All of these instruments were built according to the specific characteristics of the territories that constituted France – its mountains and forests, expansive farmlands and deep valleys.

Among those that literally stemmed from the French streets and country fairs in the medieval ages the hurdy gurdy is one. It is violently believed to have evolved from violin type instruments that Arab-Andalusian musicians brought to France through Spain. The secretary of the band turns a wheel, turning it with a crank, causing strings to vibrate — ones the musician controls by manipulating the keys. Because of its droning, deep pitch, it used to be popularly played outdoors and even used by beggars. It could equally be moved from one town to another or one region to another throughout France's towns and countryside. It had a loud clear tone with which it could play music across distances in wide expanses of geography. The early hurdy-gurdy, the earliest form of string instrument, began in the Medieval period and eventually transformed into a more complex form in the eighteenth century, by popularity amassed across the country.

The bagpipes have their roots in France too and apparently date back to at least the thirteenth century. Formerly, the bellows were filled with air which applied pressure on the piping that made the sound, of French bagpipes. They were coarse, and raucous, and were attributed to the shepherds from numerous rural areas of France who used them to entertain themselves while tending to the cattle or goats. Bagpipes were handy to be carried around and loud enough required by the shepherds who were outdoor most of the time. From the province of Brittany and Burgundy over Auverge and Provence bagpipe melodies reverberated through the woods and fields as shepherds tended their flocks. Unfortunately, from the numerous pieces of the ancient bagpipes, only a selection of them remained from the 17th century. There were other versions in the other centuries, and they also had the French legacy after them.

The vielle is a bowed string instrument, a precursor for the violin family developed in medieval France. It had five strings and a chromatic fretted fingerboard and obtained its timbre from arco bow and manual diagrams. Before roads were constructed in rural France the people lived apart from each other they held gatherings inside homes, taverns or barns for entertainment with vielle players giving active music for events, celebrations or for dancing. It added cheer to understated small country constructs as the citizens danced and celebrated. Vielles were an essential element of the instrumentation of blind and poor vagrant musicians from town to town in France earning their sustenance through charity or meager wages. Due to the capability of their Instruments called vielles to be portable and easily adaptable, these musicians managed to get a living, which was not an exception for musicians all around France.

A type of flute, the simple transverse flutes that are made of wood, were existent from as early as the Middle Ages in the French region. They were linked with shepherds and agriculturists of the countryside who idly played them on pastures or fields. The simple flutes that could be created from easily accessible raw materials such as elder or bamboo, were found in the French forests and countryside. Their light and open notes boosted morale of the labourers at the close of the day. Another hunting weapon was flutes used by hunters including poachers who employed their sharp sound in trapping wildlife. Musicians on tours carried flutes to towns where spirited gig and dance tunes kicked up further in coarse village inns after flute tunes activated country spirits. Ideally, the manageableness and the availability of early flutes coincided with leisure activities that cut across geographical differences throughout France.

Musical instruments such as hurdy-gurdy, bagpipe, vielle and flutes have been seen in medieval cities, labouring in distant mountainous regions, or any other place. They offered emotional connections that were able to engage people from different communities during the celebration, mourning, romance and play. However, more polished derivatives of some of these instruments were developed for classical use by professional musicians and musicians of culture but the raw and primitive type of construction of these original instruments shaped the image of French folk music. The local conditions of the France regions including geographical environment, climate and physical culture fostered the choral range of the French traditional musical instruments. It sustains their existence to warm up the connection of France to its origin and this is a core. From one generation to the next the old traditional instruments reflect the soul of the land in which they were forged generations ago.

France has always had local pagan and folk beliefs that have resonated through many years within its music. In pre-Christian times Celtic and Gallo-Roman paganisms formed the main beliefs of the people. These nature based religions were a cut above involving Gods and goddesses associated with the earth, seasons and farming. Music and dance normally had major importance in religious ceremonies and other functions.

When Christianity extended into the sector it did not eradicate these entrenched pagan traditions. However, a number of the shamanistic expressions of local folk remained with others adopting Christianity but integrating aspects of it and prehistoric folklore, music, and dance performances. Obviously, some motifs and images of secular music can mingle both pagan and Christian elements, and in relation to this – the traditions of the French-Folk music that appeared during the years can be described.

For instance, in the region of Brittany on the Atlantic coast of France, invoking the Celtic past, the local religious crespi or performances of 'mystery and miracle' plays which re-enacted Bible stories introduced into those plays characters and motifs borrowed from Celtic myth and tradition; Some of the pagan rites that went into other circle dances (such as gavotte and ridée for example) have Christianity put in later years to make it easier to see what it was about. The bombards and bagpipes used in the energetic dances which people listen can also relate to older Breton musicianship.

Arguably, Provence in southern France has been a cradle of Greeks, Romans, Celts and Germans. Morris dancer troupes of the region originate from pagan agricultural hailing sex fertility of Spring. Such characters as the Roi de l'Oiseau may be post-Celtic but pre-

Christian characters correspond to the folk entities that guard crops and animals. Still, such characters as Herod and Miter also appeared as masks in the traditions at that time. The lively pipe and tabor which can be still heard in Provencal dance music go back to the rustic pagan song.

Both branle, a courtly French folk music dance, and festive bourree, have had their roots in pagan circles that welcomed seasons or deities. The seventy-two more whimsical and more paced songs of French barns and village dance recall these earlier times when rites such as these grounded the barn, the village, and its people in cosmic order. Carols and Christmas hymns enthralled local polytheistical traditions and traditions like the French folk character Père Noël.

There are also some French instrumental music which have pagan connections. Medieval with virtuosity and played by the troubadours singing secular songs of nature, love, myth and adventure closely associating with the Gaelic bardic tradition eminently derived from the druidic oral tradition. In fact, even the strangulated tunes of horns and bagpipes filling the countryside at night, are blamed on Gualish or Breton gods such as Lugh using the trees to convey. Perhaps most famously, Celtic beliefs about spirits in specific trees – tree spirits, for example, or various forms of fey including the famous forest fairies that inspire so much of our modern romanticization of Nature – are enacted in impressionist composer Claude Debussy's "Prelude to the Afternoon of a Faun."

Of course, the imperative cyclical work of harvesting wheat, grapes and olives for bread, wine and oil relates French folk songs to paganistic Christian miscegenation as well. Those joyous dances, which express the participants' gratitude to the gods for the return of long days, or plaintive melodies associated with the darkness of winter, are, in essence, related to mood and feelings associated with heathen outlooks on the gifts of nature. Singing to homes for sweets and treats or money including caroling door to door has Celtic Samhain origins.

The full old Gallo-Roman calendar stuffed with gods controlling roads, rivers, cattle, houses, and health also helped shape folk airs celebrating rural realities vividly. For instance, Lugus bundling harvest, sun, arts, and oaths echoes in copious wedding speeches and poetic musings about fruitful French vineyards during the Lugnasadh time of year.

Of course, the great religious music of the Christians cannot be ruled out in creating French culture as well. But undoubtedly, great impressions were left by cathedral hymns and magnificent masses in church. But the pagan influence and mythological beasts are manifested in rainspouts in the form of gargoyles in Notre Dame, in the fancy dress of Carnaval in Nice, and in mysterious chants sung by shepherds in the Pyrenees Mountain.

In French folk music the links between past and present are constructed by way of melody, poetry, costume and lore, sacred sounds of both pagan and Christian offer a spiralling of intertwined traditions. Round dances with a soil base, singing in unison to human pulse, plaintive pipes yearning heavenward, all narrating chronicles of saints defeating mythological creatures infusing the culture, geography and history of the region.

Whether listening to the medieval Ballad of Love, Springs Awakening or the Dance from Britanny, filled with land and sky creatures, or the Grande Messe des morts, a roaring requiem for life, remember that France brings together the old traditions and new practices, pagan and Christian. The creativity, community and continuity associated with the nocturnal landscape persist at the heart of France's unique gypsy flavoured folk music for centuries. Of course, the various rituals, lyrics, and instruments may well have preserved and recontextualized sounds, histories and signs from elder religions associated with France's forests, farmlands and waters yesteryear.

Diversity and Identity

Located in the leisure of France's border there are majestic Alps and Pyrenees that have mentored the people settled in the regions. Sometimes melding into the already established musical traditions these montane people developed rich and unique patterns of music that have become threads in the French cultural fabric that reflect life in countryside areas surrounded by mountains that soar high with snow caps.

Running down the eastern part of France, the Alps represent a unique musical that is as diverse as it is influenced by mountainous living. The singularly authentic type of alpine music is, of course, the yodel – defined by the sudden transition between chest and head voices. Originating as ways of communicating short messages between socially isolated valley communities, yodels later developed into a rich vocal art form that incorporated different elaborate styles to the assemblies of the corresponding valleys' respective identities.

From this area in the heart of the French Alps, traditional yodelling merges with the monotone of the accordion and the brands of alphorn. Such musical instruments provide the oxygen that supports Alpine social functions with the benchmark of regional heritage. The accordion is small enough to carry anywhere and is the sound that sets the beat for spirited national dances—such as the schuhplattler or ländler—a dance which brings people together in dancing together. The longer version of the instrument makes sounds that imitate the alpine meadows or landscapes of the countryside in general. For this purpose the hurdy-gurdy serves well, wheel and string crank added, as an eerie back-to-the-ancients effect.

This is total diversification in the musical chatting reflecting the regional diversification per se. Songs of labour give an account of working that follows herding and farming, and the beautiful love ballads and cradle songs offer a snapshot into sharing tender emotions of mountain living.

Neighbouring Pyrenees, a different audible culture has evolved because of the French-Spanish Transition. Pyrenean music is very much vocal-oriented and comprises a harmonized polyphonic style of singing and improvised response and intervention refrains. The lyrics and tunes are more often passed messages of love, suffering and struggle focusing on human life in the harshest Terrains of the mountains. Being in the tradition of gypsy, Provencal, and other tales, the folk songs of French highlands are an accompaniment to the states of happiness, sorrows and the spirit of the Alpines and Pyrenees.

Musical instruments as well as melodies of the Pyrenees area can be considered to express the historical and artistic background and identity of people living in the elevated territories. One particular is the boha, a bagpipe as tradition has it from the region of Gascony. The kind of folk tunes that could be of the valley, and the sad, mournful tone that the drones sicken to, while the chanter plays. Tambourin à cordes, is a stringed drum made of a hollowed wooden shell with strings stretched over it and played from one end using a drum stick, contributes to the rhythmic drive and percussive pulse of the music making feet stomp during_circle dances. There is also the need for the violin, whose high pitched melodies and glorious embellishments give class to the songs and dances along side communal.

It will be observed that music is an integral component of Pyrenean society, and culture. Celebrations, prayer meetings, weddings, barn raising—each offer times those people gather to sing in groups as they get together for a common cause for praising and endorsing a similar set of ethical values. The pastourelle, a courting game, is as representative of this as when the peasants join hands and dance round in circles while spinning. In the process, they also teach songs as well as dances to their children passing on the cultural heritage of one generation to another.

While the distance is long and desert, the connection between the Pyrenees traditional music and other regional alpine systems like the Alps exists. Both are influenced by the spectaular mountain scenery, closed-off valleys, and the peasant's temporality. Contemporary tunes of Pyrenean bagpipes or Alpine yodelling and alphorns this kind of love to feel high country. They speak from the perspective of mountains and the human beings dwelling in the region. Though striking the difference from each other, the mountain music of these regions is a call of home-sickness, of the love of the soil, of the fight to live in a hard but lovely country.

The growing presence of modernity in the alpine and Pyrenean cultures puts in front of new trials a rooted musical identity of mountains. Globalization and advance in technologies have especially changed the cultural boundaries, which challenge young people to embrace modern civilization by moving more to urban areas and embracing international music. But as the culture changes and manufacturing advances, Alpine and Pyrenean folk styles are changing, adding their own to the formation of France's exquisite music.

In the last few years, Alpine and Pyrenean music have regained popularity, which is proven by various fests, master classes and projects for the preservation of regional cultures' musical intonations. Both musicians and scholars regard such traditions as important not only for their historic importance but also for their penchant to embody contemporary artistic and creative expressions of culture. The Shaw mobile symphony of sounds presents diverse narratives of mountainous folk culture that illustrate the tenacity of the ways in which a country's resilient ethos fashions the French landscape. Despite the constantly developing modern world which challenges traditional values such as alpine and Pyrenean songs unique cultural values and creativity of the motif remain unchallenged.

Just south of the English Channel and stretching along the dramatic Atlantic coast of France lies Brittany, or Breizh as people who live here prefer to call it. The sine-located peninsula is the home of the Celtic culture in France, where people still keep traditions and customs that are traced back to the days of ancestors. If there is one domain where this reality is particularly obvious it is the musical tradition which Brittany has preserved from the Celtic past through beautiful and often mystifying tunes that still live in the hearts and pulses of a community that is as proud of its roots as it is of its checkered genealogy which links it to the people of the British Isles.

Brittany's musical heritage had its roots put down almost eleven centuries ago in the early Middle Ages when Celtic tribes migrated to the continent disseminating their rich stock of folk culture into the populace. It was thus launched on its course by the seeds which immigrant folk singers originally superposed on this specifically Breton folk music, slowly maturing into its unique art that is as deeply rooted in ancient Gaelic modes of singing, as it remains organically creative and progressive in its form. When people analyze the musical culture of Brittany they go straight to the world where traditions of today meet traditions of long ago, where the pride of celts remains eternal and music makes the youth succeed. Whether beautifully haunting songs elaborate sailing songs, or noisy Guelaguetza songs, and has always been one of the key indicators of Breton culture and an exquisite link to its remote past on the shores of the British Isles.

It is at the center of Breton music the most ancient tradition of the so-called 'kan ha diskan', an acrobatic form of singing call and response. In this social performance, two singers sing a Passionate musical conversation – one singing the high tune, the other providing a countermelody. These are creations of love, work, country life and the spirit of Breton in lyric coupled with music often in the Breton language.

The instrumental traditions of Brittany also bear the hall mark of the Celtic origin of the region and innovative thinking. The biniou bagpipes sound like solemn and descant humming melody, which among other things, creates a background to folk tunes. The powerful, loud bombarded double reed announces the cheerful dances of the countryside with its tone forerunner. The poetry of the Celtic harp reflects the primitiveness of the bardic tradition; the whisper of the notes is dear to Breton music. From the collective nature of kan ha disk to such idioms as biniou and harp, Breton music explores the ethnicity of the region - the sound connection between the landscape's history and its contemporary life.

Breton music is as varied as the geographical area stretching from the tip of the Cotentin Peninsula in Normandy to the cliffs of the Landes down the west coast of France and the history of the region's Celts. Songs like those of work imitate the pace and cadence of farm and sea: the daily grind and community of rural people. Love songs describe the beauty of loneliness and loss, but also, of relationships between people, while, gentle's songs rock babies to sleep, as has been done for generations. Happy dance songs are common every day at festivals and weddings, celebrations of Breton's life.

Breton music is also associated with pre-Christian celebrations, the main among which are position celebrations of the change of seasons, such as the midsummer night Fest-Noz with fire-opening and rejoicing until morning. Here, the biniou-frequin bagpipe offers aromatic fragrances noted by the oboe-like bombard and the rhythmic accordion to power old circular steps. These meetings are all reminiscent of Brittany's archaic together and through this music they serve to revitalize the tribal spirit as songs and new melodies are passed from one generation to the other. However much the modern music of Brittany may be Americanized, raw, primitive power of it, reminiscent of its Celtic heritage never loses its charm. Whether it is a working song, a love song or a dance tune it presents in many voices the story of a nation of seafarers and moorlanders and their artistic heritage.

Although Brittany's musical tradition is far from being over and progressive, the evolution of this genre has been constantly progressing through centuries relying on the Celtic basis. Breton music from medieval times was known as the 'lai', which is just a poem with songs and tales of love and daring. Favoured by nobility in Western France, complex and allegorical 'lai' involved the concept of French troubadourism and they touched the themes centred upon Breton Myths and fables.

In later centuries, these classical trends of the royal French court were assimilated within the Breton idiom, as were the trends growing out of Baroque and renaissance. But when it introduced new influences idiosyncratic components that defined Breton music as a subgenre, traditional instrumentation, rhythms, and prehistoric melodic motifs were a form of cultural defiance that was uneasily antiusable. This was especially great since it proved that outside stimuli could be assimilated without erasing a large number of great inherited musical concepts.

Later still developments in industrialisation and urbanisation challenged traditional Breton culture from the last third of the nineteenth century. These processes threatened well set lifestyles based on agriculture and seafaring, the correlated music however, bravely adapted to the dynamic environment. Breton music, though, having some innovations with passing time, was not only preserving the affiliation with the Celtic genre but also attracting additional listeners.

Collectively, there has thus been much external pressures shaping the Bretons' musical tradition through assimilation of extra influences alongside retention of cultural roots of each generation. Such a character make it a unique artistic medium that has been able to last for many centuries deep and still in touch with the people.

The 1970s marked a significant period of Breton folk music revival spear headed by alchemist Celtic harpist Alan Stivell. They wanted to bring back new life into the history of musical Breton as proven through the integration of protracted custom and modernity. This led to the creation of fresh and exciting form that people in Breton sought to embrace and certainly rekindle interest.

A living of the centuries-long traditional acceptance of Celts living in the regions of France, this Breton revival is powered by its harmonious intricacies, forceful beats and passionate lyrics. This tradition is a direct continuation starting from the kan ha disk and up until modern Breton melodies from the 1970s, but reaching within the ancestors. For this is far more than musical instruments to the Breton people, they are the voices of Breton identity that are still alive today.

Analyzing the history of the Provençal, we have to discuss it beginning with the Middle Ages, when Provence was the region which celebrated and actively benefited from both language and art interchanges. The Occitan poet singers known as the trouvères remain important to understanding the musical culture of Provence. Singing songs of love and chivalry together with their tunes on lutes, violins, and flutes, its complicated text and meter embodied refined courtly life as well as Occitan's diverse language tradition.

Throughout the period where cultures intermingled, performing songs and dances combined French rural instruments and military-style instruments such as Gallaudet flutes, tambourines and hammered dulcimers. Still today, traditional pieces preserved and rejoiced the Mediterranean spirit of Provence whose lyrics and beats of music preserved the French-Mediterranean synthesis.

The ancient, musical language of Occitania especially influenced the Provencal region of Southern France. One form of occitan or langue d'oc used to dominate the area. Marie's Avé imbibed provencal music with the finality and poetic significance that characteristics of lyrical tones and descriptive words contributed in part to the cause. It was often the case that the Occitan songs of the troubadours were not something for entertainment alone, but indeed sometimes they were tokens of a region's cultural heritage. They told stories of love, and the beauty of nature, they carried stories of joys and frustrations of just being alive.

In consequent centuries Provencal music further developed, enriched with French influences and at the same time, it called on Mediterranean traditions. Provence coastal position linked it through ports and trade to the Mediterranean basin which introduced to it different methods and types of musical instruments. In this case, the tambourine which is a frame drum having jingles is an example that was used to furnish rhythm on dances and merry occasions.

The farandole, a circular Provençal couples dance, or 'chain dance,' is particularly synonymous with the music of Provence. This is a dance in which the joyful, enthused dancer holds their neighbour by the hand, or in a circle or chain so they are united in the dance, and above all enjoying their dance or life. It's usually played with tambourine, galoubet flute, and accordion because they support the main beat as well as produce the tune. Dancers can alter the specific movements of the farandole with random turns and changes of direction, to negotiate spaces within a village which include streets and squares.

In melodies and rhythms with sometimes daring lyrics which translate original local experiences, Occitan has deeply penetrated Provence's musical experience throughout history. At the same time as Provence's music integrates music from other areas, it still includes set dances like the farandole and reflects customs connecting to the past and today. Thus, the music of the Occitan language is in Provençal songs and instruments as nostalgia and as joy in the moments of life.

The farandole which is a dance from Provence also brings the close association of people together. Dancing at festivals, weddings, and other ceremonies, it unites a group of people by creating a common choke of movements, turning people into a happy one big team. This traditional line dance captures funful ascriptions of life events.

As varied as the country landscape of Provence, the people's songs and the instruments depicting triumphs and trials of daily toil in the fields. The new lyrics in the work songs are a vivid account of the hardship of farming, fishing and olive harvesting. The two voices, these two inflections, are of a body trying to extract sustenance from the earth. Love songs bravely depict affection and feeling with words and music. Mothers sing with love songs sung in infancy, voices sweet to rock uncomfortable children to sleep. The same voices grow louder in a communal dance called farandole, bourrée, and rigaudon, primarily with typical steps and spirited melody. In the Provencal folksongs, these are translated into voices and actions, which are true and simple, letting the audience feel universal sorrows and pleasures. They say that Provencal traditions handed down from generation to generation of heaven and earth remain authentic in the DNA.

Musical instruments of Provence are evidence of the growth of this region as part of France while adopting the Mediterranean touch of the region. Other instruments used to augment Provencal music are: The hurdy-gurdy is a string instrument in which the tunes are produced by turning a wheel; its spooky, background-like timbre comes from folksy prehistoric culture. The violin is an important instrument as well, dancing off the highest lines providing grace and elevating the folk material.

Therefore it can be seen that Provencal music far from ever being a 'set', has continued to be a living tradition that has approached itself to the changing cultural context. The Renaissance, and Baroque periods subjected these traditions to influences of France's court and European classical music. Yet in it, an influence which had been incorporated adopted and developed was kept tied with the Mediterranean sound roots, keeping such fundamental elements as the old Provençal melodies, rhythms and instruments.

For the later part of the 19th century as well as the 20th century, modernization coupled with industrial forces seeking cultural transformations in Provence. Urbanization, however, endangered the rural lifestyle itself through food production, whether through farming, fishing or other types of local trade through practicing of craft. However, as Provence was on the move with the modernization of the West, its musical culture was not wiped off the map and actually continued to be embraced and grow through out the ages while continuing the Mediterranean tradition.

It retained its connection with its prehistoric origin while assimilating influence and change from period to period of culture and creative impact. The sounds of Provence continue to resonate with a creative fusion: traditional and experimental, French and southern European,

Aristotelian and naive. As old as the history of the region it is as unchanging as rocks of Mars and its songs are the songs of a people and a culture that survives the tides of transition.

The folk music of Provence, France also emerged at the end of the twentieth century as artists endeavoured to restore this ancient culture. Grouped under figures such as Lou Dalfin, Provençal was characterized by reestablishing old tunes and instruments in the type of the galoubet flute added into a modern rhythm. It produced an lively or contemporary melodies that generated newfound pride in Provençal tradition especially among the youths.

Today the music of Provence remains a living example of the evolution of so many cultures at once. As in the troubadour singing of old Provence – and, especially the revival of the sound – the Provencal voice reaches out loud and proud according to its own beat. These sounds of the farandole dance, these melodies of the galoubet, accompanied by the tambourines create a unique and varied musical identity of modernity and history. From real life, it is truly impressive and it is so saturated with the many seeded layers of the Provençal people's experiences. According to the parallel singing of ancient generations with the modern interpretations, Provence has its cultural heritage, and singing has made for the past mastering of which comes to life and develop today.

Social Functions

The French culture always has a music function and is part of their daily lives. For example, the many French work songs that have been used to keep time, build morale, and foster fellowship in the workplace in a myriad of situations—farming to sailing, for example, over many years now.

There is evidence of using work songs in connection with agricultural activities in the countryside from the early days. Practical uses connected with coordinating movements, and regulating the flow of work and activities, are also found in some of these tunes. Field labourers in different parts of the country had different songs of reaping or harvesting while cutting their crops, which was a swing of scythe and sickle. Likewise, the workers dancing in the course of winemaking industry would produce voice in harmony with the body movements while treading the fruits in rhythmic dance steps to crush them into pulp.

Besides its functional use, it can be assumed that work songs were endowed with social and spiritual aspects. Several individuals who come from the countrified used to share and create their own music while working together through the communal tasks and Herskovits found nostalgia and humanity to them. This communal spirit helped create bonds when workers went for long hours on their feet, fostering even greater kinship among those cutting across generations, working the same fields of France that may have belonged to their forefathers.

This tradition continues to this present generation, although more pronounced in the contemporary form in the vineyard songs of the Burgundy wine producing regions. Each year during the wine grape growing period, as the harvest prepares to begin in the early autumn, winemakers repeat previous years' call and response style vocally stimulated grape calls. An old song named La Bourguignonne plays in the vineyards to the present day.

Over the years technology has eased so many aspects of agricultural work, but there are still some areas such as commercial fishing which are still very rigorous and sometimes fatal. Here too, songs have been used as background music and cohesiveness at work. In France's Atlantic and Channel coasts, mariners and fishermen sing and chant on quayside while boating home from week or month at sea.

This tradition of musical maritime as is also old as well. The lifestyle of being placed on watch during the long evenings and nights at sea and during stormy seas created a repertoire of eerie folk ballads, sea chantees, and line calls and responses, work songs. These were essential for promoting the morale and correspondent labor, to spur crews on together. These would row in time with their oars or heave heavy nets singing stories of mythical ship voyages, chanting about Providence of Sea and the plenty in rhythmic enchantments of voices on water.

These people songs are still sung in places like Lorient and Saint-Malo since it is there that boats burdened with the catch of the Atlantic come to shore. Yet, there is music, togetherness, and love when lads are there quayside; however, melancholate songs of lads lost at work are not far away. Thus, the cult of communal togeter-ness reverberates as crews celebrate another drought free trip and recall perils endured and off-duty camaraderie now with crews current and former. They remain all 'together' with their stormy sea or bright seas ahead of them.

Similarly, French labour songs are usually accompanied by protest and political satire on the political predicament of the working people. Music at such communal congregational essential for work and entertainment presented chances to complain, imagine change and equality and convene labor unions demanding better working conditions from royal masters and industrial capitalists.

As in the example of northern French coal-mining songs describing dangers and illnesses in the mine appropriating the darkness of such a job. But lively affirmative humming in unison recalled that they were all 'fellow-toughs in the coal mines' who might one day ascend to the lamp. Likewise, most textile mills and factories had their own musical tradition for sustaining through shifts. As for women in particular they kept protesting and advocacy for workers' rights singing at the textile machines or the troughs of the laundry after work. Their songs were not just sung at the workshop level alone.

Thus across trades then, functional chanting at work throughout the ages performed multiple purposes for French collectives. Songs determined the pace and incited cooperation in the working process thus fostering friendship. This solidarity was a sort of spiritual driving force, the ability to wait out adversities bound to happen in those lines of work together. Sometimes music also provided disguised consolation and rebellion sowing the seeds of change from the fields to factories in France.

Thus, although uniform and pulsing work songs set work rhythms and united peasants at communal farm fields or fishermen in accordance with the seas, those powerful pleasong also elicited hearts and minds. Thus, as related to the people's agricultural and naval chores, work songs revealed to a listener not only the tasks to be accomplished but also the hardships, desires, and collective of workers at sea and on fields throughout centuries.

In rural regions, the form of French peasant folk music was essentially an agricultural one. For instance, while working on things that involved repetitive movements such as planting, harvesting, threshing or grinding cereals, there was always a need to coordinate the movements, or else boredom would set in. These were functional songs so lyrics and melody were not that complicated, as a matter of fact, they used a lot of repetition. Street musicians used whatever lay within their hands; musical instruments early in the social instrument such as the hurdy gurdy, bagpipes, pipe and tabor, flutes, fiddles, and simple percussion. This organic folk repertoire was a musical accompaniment to everyday work and an artistic release of rural workers' emotions.

Three scenes of peasant classes singing most often were holidays and life cycles such as weddings, baptisms and funerals. On such days it was the custom of villagers to dance the bourre, ronde and branle, and instruments employed were drums, hurdy gurdies, violins and cornemuse bagpipes. These common meetings were rather a short joy, rather a feast that was in contrast to the grind and struggle of peasant's life. The dances, lyrics, and tunings were different from one regional stye to another but were integrated into the peasant's way of life in all working-class rural France.

Urban folk music evolved from such peasants' traditions with elements of theatre along with such popular dances in Paris. Musical instruments such as lutes, guitars and mandolins were more usually used to accompany performers in public streets. Material conditions of urban life enabled the use of wit and often satirical references to events and people in songs; increased literacy levels contributed to this as well Higher literacy levels are also important: urbanized folk hybrids of Parisian music even became rather 'à la mode' among the nobility for some time in the late Renaissance; the bourgeois and peasants, however, were laughing at the aristocracy attempting to assimilate what the former considered to be authentic popular

While the average person did not receive musical training and was not able to perform in the court and chamber concerts (nor attend) private concerts, members of the French nobility and bourgeoisie did. In particular, gentlemen learned how to read music, play instruments such as the lute and harpsichord and also behave during performances, as viewers or as dilettantes. It was a sign of class intended for people to show that they were cultured and lace. By a process of what we would today call diffusion from the royal courts and noble halls to the upper class of an urban society public performances of the grand musical genres of operas, ballets and above all compositions for grand orchestration were to reach lower strata of the society commonly associated with an aristocracy.

The estrangement between French folk music and high-art music reflects the clear separation of the Three Estates of the Ancién Regime period. Musical form, content, and instrumentation all pointed to one's social status, wealth and in some cases education. This started changing during the French

Revolution and the Romantic period which Sundry depicted cleavages between different classes. With the breaking down of cultural barriers music genres also started fusing with folk influences entering, in fact, barring the barons of culture, even into compositions of Bizet and Ravel in their most famous compositions. However, the remnants of the high art-popular art divide determined the French perception of music for several decades.

In French society, for example, one appreciates like civilizing cultural opposition between 'cultured' and 'low' music to the present day. For example, modern French folk musicians, singers and dancers will incorporate traditional French music instruments such as accordions and dancing instruments, dancing beats with modern-day instruments and beats. This suggests an ongoing process of shifting blending of the local in order to identify new commonalities with elite citizens regarding topics that cross over established classes. A long glance at French music history demonstrates altogether different access and forms across societies, however, they also illustrate how no music subgenre remains untouched by the other ones, however high or low. The antagonism of court and country, high and low-ranking citizens goes on in the various beats, instrumental accompaniments, songs and seasoning that now constitute French musical pluralism. That way vestiges of past hierarchies are seen to be present yet so are signs of change which necessarily keep musical traditions alive.

Music plays an important part in French culture and traditions and is inextricably connected with significant life cycle events.

From birth to death, people in France have always used music to sanctify life phases or as a way of honouring it. It is not surprising that music has been described to be as spontaneously available at French festivities, as wine at a wedding celebration, harvest, and other rites of passage. But what has been the part of music, or of song, as traditionally involved in these rituals of life in France? It is high time that an emphasis shifted and more focus was placed on the tunes, the instruments, and the changes musical traditions associated with baptisms, weddings, funerals, and seasonal celebrations underwent over the centuries.

Baptism and Birth

Baptism is the sacrament that takes place soon after childbirth; it defines a child's membership in the Church and the community. In past years in France, they included hymns sung without accompaniment by a chorus of the congregation or nuns. Over time starting from the late 1800s up to the early 1900s, organs were used more as musicians for churches. It would also be possible to sing very basic folk songs that would be sung during the baptism party to welcome the newborn baby. According to folklore in a few areas, parents maintained a small piece of cloth that was used to wrap the newborn and had ribbons and silver charms as birth protection which was passed from the medieval ages. For French babies, as for those in other lands, it has ever been lullabies and folk songs which have dispelled the evils of night.

Wedding Customs

Songs are a very lively aspect of the French marriage rites and procreation, with astounding consistency that changing circumstances have been unable to disrupt. In Medieval France there were poet singers called troubadours and jongleurs; these were poet musicians who travelled from place to place performing at the request of the lords and at weddings people used to sing love songs. The string and wind instruments secured drive-in rhythms. This tradition persisted for centuries in peasant weddings through folk violins and, stringed hurdy gurdy instruments created merriment. Organs started at French weddings in the early 1700s but string bands for regional dance continued till the early 1900s.

Symbolic wedding songs also continued in France, as did Indeed, symbolic wedding songs also extended to France. Exiting the church as newlyweds for the receptions, children's choirs sang the agreeable 13th century round "C'est la cloche de Corneville" - the wedding bells are ringing. Lads tapped the drum with sheepskins immediately after the church ceremonies were over. At wedding feasts, howbeit, gross and filthy, groups sang rhyming couplets with good wishes for fertility and prosperity. These customs are basically followed even in the modern-day wedding where the wedding waltz at French receptions is still performed.

Funerals and Mourning

Mourning rituals in France likewise used music in their funerals even in modern day. The death knell was rung in villages of yore whenever a resident passed away; New. Additional funeral songs comprised hymns in Latin such as 'Libera me' which simply translates to deliver me Lord from the period of judgement. It was a funereal air that would ring through French churches during centuries of Requiem masses. Later the choirs had a cappella parts and instruments such as organs and orchestra bassoons.

During the funerals in early 19th century France, both the metallophones as well as the drum rolls were used to follow the cortege from the church to the graveyard. Urban church bells tolled to announce mourning wearing black sheets on the horses drawing a flower-wreathed carriage. So music, in this way, helped in expressing group mourning, and in promoting people's unity of species.

Seasonal Celebrations

Music has always erupted suddenly during annual village festivals, harvest festivals and other related occasions in France. People used bagpipes, flutes, fiddles, and drums, boys danced and marched cows and sheep beautifully dressed and adorned to bless the land before sowing the seeds. Like that of Demeter's daughter Persephone who rises from Hades in spring, olive-wreathed young shepherdesses portrayed seasonal myths. Young people in wine regions picking grapes staged the working class and sang and danced as a form of celebration of cyclical nature of life.

Celebrations of the winter solstice included groups chanting "Noeles" - old French carols and songs about the nativity spread over the fire. In Burgundy and Provence, it was the custom of travelling carol singers complete with creches in the doors singing these winter songs. Joyous music and foods of choice embellished sexual fertility summer solstice rites. Such ritual dances are represented, for example, by the Provencal "La Farandole" during which dancer moves in the winding column led by the 'masque' dressed as vines and leaves. In their melodies inherited by ancestors, the French get acquainted with cycles of death and rebirth – the turning wheel that connects all lives.

France's ritual music associate's society's recollections across the transition, from eternal Latin requiem for the martyr saints up to spirited troubadour lyrics in love, up to bardic songs to support the generations of workers during the harvest time. Whether celebrating the birth of a newborn babe or honouring couple on their wedding day, tears of grief or laughter, the variety of the melodies giving colour to such scenes preserve the cultural identity in their constant occupation over France's turbulent ages. They reflect the best of that Galtian 'thing' called joie de vivre, which is French for soul. Let the carillons of true Norman oboes break, let the auction drums of Provence in markets and the hearty tones of the bagpipes in lanes. When joy happens at the crossroads of one's existence, music and happy tunes will be the first to cut the rug.

Mythology and Legends

From stories of trolls and Knights to stories of fairies and water spirits, French storytelling is a great and wonderful experience. Of the hundreds of thousands of old stories that might no longer be told, a stunning number are still extant, preserved in song. There is no doubt that music has acted as one of the best ways of passing on the Mythological and legendary traditions of France.

Common and popular forms of grand legends singing show that telling legends is more effective when singing, not telling. That's why musicality, rhyme, and melodic lines contribute to the fact that these stories are planted deeper into the cultural memory. Songs also fit well in the practice of memorizing and passing on lore, a number of which have no written standard. Some of the contemporary ones relate to medieval French folklore or, in fact, earlier Celtic associations. Music has guaranteed that these icons as la Bête du Gévaudan or Mélusine, water fairy, continue to enchant through centuries.

The Beast of Gévaudan Roams On

One of the most well-known of these legends was the cheesy Beast of Gévaudan, which was inspired by a real beast that many claimed resembled a wolf and was responsible for the death of over a hundred people in South-Central France in the 1760s.

La Bête can still be summed up in stories and songs in the present day. In one show, the beast resembled a werewolf, and left its prey in a state of shock with rather unusual moves like head and neck biting without eating. Historical accounts indicate that famous and fearless hunters and the hunter named Jean Chastel hunted on it down just in 1767.

The barbarous acts and absence of concrete identity for the creature ensured that other people proceeded to tell a countless number of stories, which developed into legends. Music even nowadays helps the legend to persist by singing the French ballad "La Bête Féroce de la Gévaudan", which tells about the numerous murders and victory over the beast by Chastel. The Gévaudan beast is also the subject of contemporary musicians, including the rock operas of the Parks entitled 'Le Pacte des Loups' and a French hip hop tune 'La

Bête.' The story goes on as emotive song recreations of the disastrous attacks that the people had to go through two and a half centuries ago grip people's imagination.

The Water Fairy Mélusine: An Enchantment

These are legends though the legend of Mélusine lasts for even more centuries. Known as the fairy or goddess of the watery sources from the French mythology of the Middle Ages and earlier historical periods, Mélusine was. One among them says that she was changing into a serpent merely below the human body, once a week. However, resembling notes concern Mélusine employing her magical authority over water and rain for the advantage of heroes or nobles in their daring endeavours such as heaping colossal castles from base rock.

In such stories, she is connected to the House of Lusignan aristocratic family and helps Hugh le Brun in his battles if he promises not to see her on Saturday as she turns ugly. But then, perverting himself into the oath he made, he noticed the reptilian like lower part of her body. She then faded for a while from his life but remained as a spiritual guardian of Mélusine descendants. Later, several nobles incorporated Mélusine into their armoury and they used the unfamiliar words 'Mélusina Audicator,' the meaning of which is 'A Mouse that Thunders.' She gave meaning to her water spirit symbol as a virtue.

Similar to how the Beast of Gévaudan assists with the perpetuation of Mélusine's interesting obscure reputation, Story-songs include the 1990s music called "Mélusine's Song" by

Louisiana French band BeauSoleil. The words state the fairy's eternal enchantment intended for human actions of the past, the present as well as the future. It and other movies of the modern world help today's viewers to find their own link to the eternal components of humanity that gave birth to her legend centuries ago.

From Cruise to Cryptozoology, songs subsidize lore

Besides representing the totemic fauna of specific regions, in extended versed stories, which were incorporated into musicals, other legends of France were annually retold. For example, ballads about Knights and great wars during the Crusades period are partly remembered by vibrant singing renditions. The "Chanson de la Croisade Albigeoise" of the thousand two hundred and odd records a grim crusade to extinguish the heretics and incite the Christian Knighthood. Actual battles like the Siege of Carcassonne are shown along with mythical fights such as demons fighting angels in the air above. And so, such lore still continues to remain current in dramatic recitations chanted to lyrical tunes.

In the more contemporary time, songs also transmit mythological elements. Following old folklore spirits, legends about supernatural monsters are still waked up "cryptozoological" searching for mythic creatures such as Loch Ness monster, sasquatch/bigfoot. Even recent French musical groups like SetUp65 took a new twist in singing story ballads like medieval Troubadours. Their "Le Loup-Garou de Thônes" which translates to the werewolf of Thônes, is an example of the use of acoustic guitar, flute and percussion to retell gruesome werewolf incidents in French Alps. But of course, it reproduces typical features of mythic archetypes and shapes even as it adapts them to the postmodern sensibility.

The Singer and the Story

But why do melodies and lyrics so well bring the legends into cultural memory? It is possible that several key factors exist. First, the musical elements can stimulate a response that is not easy to provide through simple tellings of history. This is so because rhythm qualifies and quantifies the relationships between characters and events as instrumentations and harmonies enrich and sacralize the characters and events using the voices. It also helps in learning and also enables one to pass on accurate information without necessarily referring to the musical lyrics.

Further, the quality of story songs is improved by talented composers and performers. When talented musicians learn from mythical themes, they are capable of amplifying the source myths' elements in their artwork. As)]. Typically identified as great singers from various cultures, the appealing performer by passion and appeal brings myths into the vivid realm of the audience's imagination. Perhaps there is a primitive satisfaction in recounting stories and passion, of painting pictures by firelight or candle, of fleshing out old tales over roasts around the fire and candles on the table.

Besides, with song, the separation between the artist and listener ceases to exist as well.

Listeners who get to watch or listen to story songs usually get drawn into singing along, at least in the choruses, or feeling as if they are part of the story. This breaking down of the "fourth wall" draws the listeners in to participate instead of observe. In this way, artists, and spectators generate the living mythology and living reality of the legendary material. That small shared magic will guarantee folklore goes on to unite societies through enshrined imaginative adventure. They therefore remain strong through singing community across distances and lifetimes.

Preserving Cultural Treasures

And so from the hexed creature who terrorized Gévaudan of the 18th century to the aquatic Lady Mélusine whose presence is enough to make hearts burst with imagination,

French legends would be grateful to the art of songwriting. Forceful story-singing resurrects myths to guarantee they reach future generations. Orally handed down as folklore, simple tunes carry great fertile imaginations to the ears. These singing legends of the world help free modern minds and emotions to ride through the wonderlands of fantasy, transported from dull reality by musical time machines.

With the fast and demanding tempo of life today, ironic and grotesque these songs recall unity with origins, cycles and images. Vectors that set foot and reason in us irrespective of time and space. The singing legends also provide mental solace to some extent in imaginative worlds other than ordinary problems. On many aspects, these enshrinements of musical myths continue to serve fundamental human needs. Duly the

French legends endure always bolstered forward by catchy tunes and strongly rhymed lyrics that bear them on, through the ages, waiting for susceptible minds and roving dreams to yield to the spell of the lyrics.

Centuries of oral tradition, folklore and leavings of ancient pagan beliefs intermixed with Christian, has long shaped the French rural psyche as one believing in the supernatural and magical. From the rich tapestry of beliefs, the folk music of France, especially of the countryside stands forth with songs and stories of fairies, werewolves, witches, ghosts and the rest and the mighty forces of the curse and the blessing.

The fairy or fée is one of the most famous supernatural figures in French folk music. These are these magical beings, frequently described as beautiful and ethereal woman who holds great power and dwell in enchanted realm away from the mortal one. The French folk repertoire abounds in songs and tales about fairies, and these narratives usually fall into the enchanting, even love storys, or the cautions about what happens when you run into these otherworldly creatures.

The second is the werewolves (loups-garous), recurring as a supernatural motif in French folk music. These shapeshifting beings — thought to turn from humans into wolves with the sight of the moon at full — have a long history of fascination and fear in French rural imagination. Often, when we hear tales and songs about werewolves, we see it being about transformation as him becoming a beast or the curse on him or the fight between him and the human side of him.

The song "Le Loup-Garou" (The Werewolf) is a striking example of a French folk ballad that delves into the dark and mysterious world of the werewolf. It's a tale of a man cursed to transform into a werewolf and wander the country side by an insatiable blood hunger. Eerie melody and chilling lyrics of the song describe the primal fear and terms of awe the song makes one feel for what the werewolf is, as well as tragic effect of the curse through which the man is bound to his fated beast.

Another figure of French folklore that appears in French folk music is witches or sorcières. To the barbarian, however, these powerful beings are potentially malevolent, indeed at times they are even malevolent, and it's thought they can cast spells, brew potions and commune with the forces of darkness.

Regardless of whether witches are always bad or do good, often it is about power and temptation and the consequences of digging in the dark arts.

The song "La Sorcière" (The Witch) is a captivating example of a French folk ballad that delves into the enigmatic and dangerous world of the witch. It is the story of a young woman accused of witchcraft who is tried. She protests her innocence but is condemned to burn at the stake, here she is the poster child for what can happen if you are looked upon as a witch in a superstitious afraid community.

Recurring motifs in French folk music are ghosts and spirits, a testimony to a strong belief in the supernatural and in the ghosts or spirits able to influence the living. Ghosts Songs and Tales often lurch from loss, leading to the uncertain boundary between the worlds of the living and the dead.

The song "Le Revenant" (The Ghost) is a poignant example of a French folk ballad that delves into the ethereal and haunting world of the ghost. This melancholic tune tells the story of a young man who came back from the dead to visit his beloved but to her grave, she has moved on and married another. The haunting notes of the song are accompanied by lyrics that with reflect the ghost story: about what relationships are, what they are not, what survives when we take them away.

French folk music is concerned with the supernatural power of cursing and blessing, which are areas seen to hold the ability to exercise a strong influence on the life of a person. These powerful magics are sung and told in songs and stories; covering topics related to predestination, choice, and the other side of the coin.

For instance, the French folk music song called 'La Malédiction' or 'The Curse' could also be something of a curse. It is about a man punished by a vengeful spirit to go wandering the face of the earth, suffering. There's a periphery to this song, which is quite emotive, and words say that the listeners are full of the hatred and the curses and how those whoever gets cursed never knows the outcome due to the mystery attached to those curses.

Not only to describe the manifestations of the esoteric, French folk music also used it in a practical way, namely in the various rites that exist to command these and similar "occult phenomena." In fact the songs and chants are believed to have magical properties; that the tune and words of the songs and chants can alter supernatural outcomes to specific effects.

In "Chant de Guérison" (Healing Song), readers see that a French folk tune is usable in magical ways, like healing. This undulating, monotonous chant sung at rituals is held to have healing powers to wipe out disease; to exorcise evil; and to adjust the physical structure of man and his spirit. Lavender coloured pop with lyrics that have a soothering quality, it does well to embody the concept of the healing properties of music and the paranormal.

The setting's folklore in French folk music is exhibited by supernaturalistic components whether as representations of occult muses or praxeologically functional as offering ceremonial aspects. And now one can see straightforwardly that such songs as 'La Malédiction' and 'Chant de Guérison' reveal how this literary tradition enters into the core of the imprecations, blessings, and the mystical forces of morality, ritual and occult.

While the supernatural and magical elements of French folk music are certainly the result of some wild fantasy and a little bit of imagination, these are actually cultural practises, the roots of which stem from the folk beliefs and practises that have defined and sustained these traditions. These songs and stories are a way of making sense of the mysteries and unknowable that constitute the world, exploring the disquiet and mysterious and getting closer to the deep and unchanging forces that lie outside the ordinary.

The melodic and enchanting phrases and leitmotifs of French folk songs provide a direct key into a culture which is sensitive to natural rhythms and the allure of magic — here curses co-exist with cats, fairies, werewolves, and sorcerers. That is the music of the supernatural and magical, a rich tapestry of the human imagination, the power of the human imagination, as it weren't for the faltering imagination endured by the human race when it comes to the worlds beyond the corporeal.

Three of the major mythological creatures found in France are fairies (fées) witches (sorcières) and werewolves (loup-garous). While the subjects of these motifs have been transmitted from one generation to another in forms of folklore stories, they have been converted into poetic texts of songs in French music in general and in all the major music genres in particular.

Fairies

Thus, fairy occupies an unstable and rather dual position within the French imaginary landscape – sometimes it may seem to be good, magical figure associated with the activity of the other world rather than evil supernatural figure connected with paganism. The first references to them in the French literature up to their origin are linked to the 12th century in the poetic writings of Marie de France. In the next centuries, fairies were adopted as common characters in fables and legends of all French regions.

Given that fairies are still an omnipresent signifier across collective myth, it was only a matter of time before it emerged in French music. Pre-renaissance French Folk ballads like Si les fées n'existaient pas or translated as "If Fairies Didn't Exist" where basically asking if there is such thing as fairy creatures in society. In more contemporary style, fairies, Véronique Sanson usually sings the song 'La Fée' (The Fairy), which means magical charm. However, in 'La Légende du Roi Arthur' a rock opera that tells the legend of King Arthur, the fairies symbolize the spirits which predestine the character's destinies. Different fairy shown in this musical is as such to illustrate the versatility of this archetype in the fairy tales.

Witches

Witches also had prior representation in French literature extending back through hundreds of years and are referred to as sorcières in French fables and folklore. They knew the cure for the diseases, charms and powers; but, per folklore, witches were pagan soul-traders who made deals with the devil akin to the black magic and wickedness.

In music, witches seem more like charming spirits than any evil doers. For example, taking the reputation of witches to ridiculous level, Georges Brassens sings "La Sorcière", while giving vigor and power of witches' midnight flight, Bratsch's "La Sorcière de Minuit". Some of those are, Michel Polnareff's "La Sorcière" that portray witch characters as sexual fantasies. Through the prisms of creative reinterpretations of the history of witch folklore, these characterizations vary in how they reinterpret.

Werewolves

Werewolves or loup-garous transform human beings into wolves and struggle with animalist instincts while trying to keep human minds.Loups garou cannot be discussed independently of European but the French version seems closer to human and thus more distinct as they can turn back into humans later.

This motif is less frequent in French music compared to fairies or witches, but there are certain opuses that belong to that theme. From this transformation, comes the titular overcame (werewolf) protagonist of Jacques Higelin's rock song 'Le Loup Garou'. It bespeaks the psychic disturbance which this metamorphosis involves. For example, Anorexia Nervosa's Le Loup et le Soleil (The Wolf and the Sun) is the Werewolf lament. Both songs therefore utilize the werewolf to try and make sense of some of life's biggest questions of the human experience.

Lasting Motifs

Fairies, witchcrafts, and werewolves capture human imagination and many a time turn into literary characters and I argue that their endurance has facilitated their transition from verbal folklore into musical scores across genres and eras. In some cases, they symbolize whimsical dream, in other – magical knowledge, sometimes they act as mysterious and sexy ladies, and in others they embody people's hardships disguised as terrifying creatures. That these mythic motifs endure in French music marks them as more than objects of cultural fantasy and imagination; they are evidence that the impulses which created them remain assured of their ability to continue to do so. It also shows how the mythical beings in them have the fluidity provided for them being passed through the ages of storytelling and song, artists of other generations succeeding them give their own connotations and interpretations.

Medieval and Renaissance

The medieval period has its own colourful place in the musical history of France primarily because of cultural interactions resulting from the activities of the troubadours and jongleurs. These poets were musicians hailing from different areas of France but nevertheless propagated widespread theories of music and assimilated otherwise spelled cultures. Their timeless artistic inventions made connections between the masses and tied them to harmony of sound that can still be heard to the present.

Troubadours in turn were the evolutionary offspring of poets, the latter being an offshoot of Occitan speaking territories of the Aquitaine, Provence and Languedoc which spread in the late 11th and early 12th centuries. Usually composed by people of noble birth, they wrote in langue d'oc, which created the poetry of courtly love, social scandal and chivalry. Rotational patterns are dense compared to free metered poems, while cansos celebrated the philosophies of love as well as humility for a higher class of nobility through lyrics. While noble, troubadours acted as carriers of unity seeds that moved from one feudal court for another, sharing songs depicting unity in a melancholic way.

On the other hand, the jongleurs developed from low birth origin aluminated persons who roamed around the country performing the cansos. These musicians and storytellers ensured that the polite airs of the troubadours saturated the ranks of feudalism and beyond and so, the movement crossed geographic lines without rupturing the fabric of the culture. Together, the troubadours and jongleurs offered Occitan as a language of literature and the streets, as well as language and culture. Their music strung together the fine tapes which connected one person to the next through the culture we now know as 'French', while their home language may not have necessarily been the same. In integrating exchange and innovation into melodies their songs were sounding out through the century and are still resonant across time.

The term 'troubadours' is most often connected to southern France and the Occitan speaking countries but was more widespread in its influence. While singing those songs and presenting new artistic ideas in the northern Kingdoms, the troubadours served in a way, as envoys of southern musical and poetic culture. As far as new musical styles and formation are concerned, they have changed the image of the country's music through their imaginative creations of tune, rhythm and poetic structure.

From Old French "trover" meaning 'to compose,' their counterparts in northern France were the trouvères. The trouvères were particularly rooted in the southern tradition; they borrowed troubadour features of poetic and musical practice and contributed to sharing them throughout the north.

As with their high-born counterparts, the trouvères sang to the medieval nobility. Their chansons ranged from cover topics such as love songs, pastourelles or shepherdess songs, to heroical chansons de geste. Hence, while the southern elements are mixed with the Northern innovations, the trouvères' art was instrumental in the actualization of the significant French musical characteristics in interaction with diverse regional features, which built up the national culture.

It was to this court that the troubadours, who had learned and brought up southern melodic and poetical cultivation, carried their songs. Such a reliance was most dependent on the idea that the northern trouvères were able to comprehend and absord other forms, both poetic and musical, into their own works. Each entertained nobility as minstrels, the troubadours in the development of traditions characteristic to specific regions of southern Occitan and the trouvères in the formation of Northern French tradition with such influences. Thanks to those, the beginning of creative work formation in the medieval France entered frame while regional peculiarities existed.

The jongleurs here turn out to be an important method of circulation of the texts of troubadours and trouvères in medieval France. While the noble troubadours and trouvères sang fine poems and songs the jongleurs were of all societal strata. They moved from one village to the other entertaining the nobilities and the public through songs and dance, juggling, and acrobatics display.

There are jongleurs who took three basic forms of the tales of troubadours and trouvères and recast them for the people. In sordid drinking hole, and the thronged bazaars and noisy piazzas, they brought passion and energy to the complex and elegant songs. Therefore the jongleurs were able to link the sophistication of troubadour lyricism and songs to the realities of the common man. Its S for spectacle combined music, poetry and entertainment and made available hitherto enclosed courtyard forms of art to a broad audience.

French music today carries its mark of the role of troubadours, trouvères and of jongleurs. The arbitrary and poetic virginities introduced by rumours and trouvours seated an opulent ground used by posterior stages of music. as well as operas and ballets of the Baroque period. However, such song traditions of French verse were not just limited to courting, for medieval troubadours to contemporary interpreters placed an everlasting lyrical persona into French music.

Among the poets and performers who really did manage to play a major role to preserve and spread the French language and its literature are troubadours, troubadours and jongleurs. In fact, their Occitan and Old French songs and poems contributed positively towards the standardization of those two vernaculars, and therefore the start of a proper French tradition.

The French bourgeoisie's impact was not only limited to France but they were affecting musical and literary customs among other regions. It exercised much influence upon the Sicilian School of poetry in Italy and the Minnesang, in Germany, and kindred poetry. Thus translated and adapted, the songs and verses of the troubadours and trouvères became the vehicle for transmission of art and culture of Europe wide proportions. However, the activities of these French artists in the growth of local languages and the extension of their cultures are critiqued in only 169 words.

The sacral music derived from the Gregorian chant occupied the apex of the culture, it played an acephalous role as religious music during the church performance.

Ecclesiastical music was a pure expression of the Church's total control over medieval life – a relation indicative of ecclesiastical music's function. Before and after the introduction of the Gregorian chant, the liturgy was formed by monophonic textures and Latin rites. That is the dancing by clergy and monks to encourage a divine rapport during the mass. The mihi coursework of the Council of Trent in the sixteenth century circumscribed music's instructive responsibilities in regard to adoration, fearful of the fiasco of comprehensibility. Such a rigorous categorization of sacred forms of the song brought in constant conflict with secular songs from paganism remnants or burgeoning theaters and bardic traditions regarded as an immoral diversion from devotion.

While this may have been the case, secular folk innovations persisted in seeping themselves into ecclesiastical forms. This, of course, stemmed from the smart strategies of composers and performers that understood the beloved tunes' impact on parishes. For example, pith and choruses interwoven into hymes copied secular frames at the same time as litigious words conveyed religious meanings. Such synthesizing creative strategies served to increase the diffusion of musics, at the same and reinstate the Church's control over the soundscape through renewals of selected secular innovations, thus preserving the church's hegemonic hold on cultural reproduction.

Secular medieval folk songs were all therefore in striking opposition to the mannered world of religious compositions. These lively songs were sung not in serious churches but on the streets, this noisy and, in many instances, rowdy peasant society of Medieval Europe. The humanities of troubadours, trouvères as well as numerous jongleurs enriched the figures of speech and color of the art of the Middle Ages and early Renaissance through singing lay-brokens, ballads, verse and prose in satisfying the taste for romance and the realistic warmth of affection, the beauty of the appeal of nature and the impression of everyday realism.

Folk music however can be traced back to the largest tribal conventions where it was performed at festivities, dances, celebrations, etc. Most of such compositions depicted themes of love, eroticism and materialism- issues that rebelled against the doctrines of the Church. This music which lies in the human domain opposed this and offered a different way from what the church was trying to invoke: to stay focused on the spiritual. Whereas sacred music sang its hymns to the lords of heaven, medieval secular folk tunes spoke the songs of regular folks and rang through the community in the persistence of medieval folk music culture.

But sacred and worldly music were rivals, although the Church took secular songs: they could produce a response from Christians.

This was expressed in several ways. Liturgeal drama had some complications – some about allowing the use of vernacular languages and tunes that were familiar to allow a more effective transmission of religious messages. Hymns and carols to combine spiritual messages with strongly developed folk elements which allowed producing un-pretentious, entertaining songs. This music became more and more folklike, the rhythms and melodies of processional songs encouraging celebration and, in effect, music as the use of music to bring people together. Formerly hostile, the Church realized that there was a social and motivational quality to folk music that can be incorporated into the liturgy. The ordinary, the tuneful, and the lively identified with congregations, and even sacred texts were given to people in a less sombre, more reassuring tone. This integration enlivened worship, popularized doctrine, and increased spiritual synergy between Church and the common congregation using song. The secular notes, however, rose; profane was found capable of vibrating devotionally, and the Church shouted its decision with a unanimous clap: the profane could yet make the souls travel their distances towards divinity.

They accompanied the relationship between the church and worldly music during the French music period. Both sacred and secular themes were used frequently as sources of inspiration for the artists who were attempting to combine these two styles. Their compositions represented combining of genres and topics that transcended most of the standards.

This dynamic tension and adaptation was one of the most important factors mentioned in determining the course of French composition. The people were involved in the church services because hymns, also in folk rhythms and melodies were adopted to make services exciting. Similarly, production of religious themes in non-religious works linked people through common feeling. Eventually, two styles starting from the 14th century created a base for the new musical forms, where church and popular elements combining produced the mosaic-like polyphony of the 14th century Ars Nova and the close and elegant but complex chansons of the Renaissance.

Of course, the interchange of the two, of the sacred and secular, was fundamental to the construction of France. The sacral and profane imagery of medieval music together with its sacral and profane imagery games gloriously strengthens the idea of art as a unity of arts on the part of diverse parts in art which were provided to him. The blending of music of the spheres and of valleys and hills, festive as well as bitter, within a massive cathedral or a joyful country fair produced solidarity. THIS integration produced astonishing ingenuity and satisfied the souls and sensitivities of all the classes as to their religious requirements and their artistic preferences. The amalgamation of genres created a common, persistently basic foundation for French culture that lasted for several generations from Medieval mystical and scholarly organum to the vibrant and perambulatory trouvères singers. Consequently, the continuity of luxury, playfulness, and religiosity of the French music can be credited to the functioning of the productive synergy between the sacred and the profane convention.

The Renaissance in France was a revival of that masterpiece of the arts that was evident in all aspects of societal life. It consisted of a rich culture in music and dance that was informed by royal etiquette, among the Lowcountry bawdiness. Major dances of the Renaissance such as branle, bourrée, pavane and galliard have their roots in relatively simple country dances, danced in the rural areas. As their rhythms were defined and enshrined in the academy, their fast tempos and apparent cheeriness spoke of origins in the bucolic simplicity and freedom of folk culture.

An example is the branle that included lines of dancers with hand-in-hand moving as one as they step. Originally devised for weddings and fairs in the medieval countryside, this vigorous dance linked High Renaissance nobles to the very sort of mutual fellowship which peasants had known. Similarly, the rather energetic and brisk dancing pattern of the quick hops and performing rhythmic tempo of bourrée originates from the countryside of Auvergne and gained the reputation of the favourite fair and market dance. Through such folk forms, the same songs that united people in villages became incorporated into the aristocratic schemes of life.

The French Renaissance was a time of great cultural renaissance in which such social equality through dance was a regular aspect. In tempo and melody, the pavane and galliard are again associated with courtly grace and, in their performance, with that lower-class coarseness found in some of the folk tunes. Covering different classes dancers danced together these songs and united in mutual joviality. In Renaissance, the music and dance were so bright and lively that the brightness and vivaciousness could be due only to the fact not that of hardly the skill or complexity in music or dance, or it would form music or choreography, but people and their celebration is everywhere in the frames of that era surpassed in all the rolls of society.

During the course of the Renaissance, rustic dance like El branle and El bourrée were introduced in the peasant village and migrated to the noble houses. Their liveliness and beat enlivened the rather stately aristocratic dances. Following are some of the factors which helped the arts transition from one culture to the other. Noble patronage was imperative since nobles required entertainment with which to assert their refined status and often 'aristocratic' spirited folk dances. Rustic dances were refined by nobles who similarly hired musicians and dancing masters who arranged, choreographed and brought style and training to the court.

In this capacity, it may be said that peasant folk dances were transformed into objects that are associated with court life. The branle was a light but appealing movement, captivating of nobles with what can be called a lively spirit. It became a favorite of the royal performers who arranged it as an entertaining performance in stuccoed halls. Similarly, the bourrée with its bristling rhythmic energy, its stylized abandon along with its lively energetic steps was a black to the elegant courtly manner of the fashionable society, thereby pleasing its elite spectators.

When the nobles started patronizing the folk arts, the respective culture of the peasant as well as the noble elite class became quite similar. In an attempt to provide pure cultures a form of upper-class spin, nobles introduced airs in raw folk tunes. In turn, peasant dances assimilated manners and stylistic features of the aristocracy and the nobility. This intermingling also created the necessary conditions for the novelty for the courts of spirited Folk dances, enlivening the court entertainments.

In Renaissance dances instruments were very important and the melodies and rhythms used in particular compositions were usually cheerful and were borrowed from folk sources. The kind of dances that accompanied or got associated with the courtly art of the Renaissance included the briar rose, sad, king's morris, neck, chickens, slaughter and the hunt. The elements of musical style included fast rhythm with samples of extended melody and major polyphonic formulas in the kit. The dance music was developed by composers like Claude Gervaise, Pierre Attaingnant and Thoinot Arbeau who drew more of the folk-dance style in compositions that spread the court dances among the people of different classes. This work turned out to be very enlightening as Arbeau's 1589 publication of "Orchésographie" furnished representations with descriptions of the dances and the music performed. Therefore, it is easy to understand how the renaissance dances could have been properly propagated by this vigorous bond that music had with dance and culture.

As with all Renaissance dances, the intricacies depicted the social structures of the society at that time. The choreographic schemes and their ritually opulent costumes performed nobility status and social stratification. The dance and opulent performances that were advertised meant that nobility was affordable and classy. In the rural villages, dances helped to build people's identity in that they danced... The blessings of the lively branle and bourrée were that it relieved commoner's monotonous humdrum life.

These folk dances gave bright and happy moments to togetherness in the midst of struggle and suffering. In addition, dances transmitted culture from one generation to the other. It was that which allowed the knowledge itself to pass on, in the form of rhythm and melody and movement, something that would have been lost for generations otherwise. Thus, dances provided the stream of culture's continuity regardless of the changes society was experiencing at that time. A versatile social function of dances is evident for both noble and ordinary people throughout the period in question. Folk dances mean folk dances were a kind of a way to slacken some of the harshness of the peasantry through song and dance. Thus, the continuation of dance traditions was now guaranteeing that memory of a culture was passed on to the generations in transition. In various ways, the functions of Renaissance dances illuminated aspects of the social culture.

The musical and the choreographical accomplishments identified with the dance music of the Renaissance have formed the framework of rhythm, melody and movement that is observable in the subsequent epochs. This movement motivated and paved the way for inferior courtly Baroque dances and modern or classical ballet and opera as well as folk material. Such blending of nobility and churlishness, of divinity and worldliness illuminates the interaction between the country and the noble tradition in the period of the Renaissance carefully. Finally, they created a legacy — a legacy of all rhythm and melody through decades, of the artistic of dance and music that became a legacy for the centuries ahead.

Music and Revolution

With deep roots in the common memory and cultural heritage of a people, folk music has always been a powerful means of expressing dissent, producing solidarity, and mobilizing communities in war and revolution. One of the French Revolution's seismic events, this revolution had left a rich ford on its tapes of folk songs which had captured the spirit of that time, expressed the people's grievances and called into line for liberty, equality, and fraternity. If we wanted to study exactly how the role of folk music played during the French Revolution and other uprisings, we would be entering the historical underworld of song which combined song with the struggle for freedom and the means of social justice, with song's power helping to amplify the voices of the oppressed, fuel the fires of rebellion.

The French Revolution, which broke out in the year 1789, was a crashing point in French history and world history. The upheaval was a complex product of a set of factors, some of them economic, others absolute monarchy, still others feudalism, and yet others the late Enlightenment ideas that had already to some degree infected French society. At the time, folk music provided the perfect soundtrack to the revolution, reflecting the aspirations, frustrations and hopes of the people at that time. While the songs of the revolution were not songs of entertainment, the songs of the revolution were not mere protest, even though they were forms of protest, they were forms of protest, but they were also powerful tools for protest, solidarity, and mobilization and they captured something of the spirit of the times and they unmoved the populace.

The French Revolution has been memorable and enduring courtesy of "La Marseillaise," the French national anthem. In its original, known as Chant de guerre pour l'armée du Rhin, written by Claude Joseph Rouget de Lisle in 1792. The tune and the words to encourage people to stand and fight tyranny and for their country became a revolutionary song. As they went to war, soldiers sang it, but workers or peasants sang it when demonstrating.

Another revolutionary cultural advance involved a kind of folk song that was 'La Marseillaise'. These were songs to put into music and song form in order to give voice to music from the experiences, grumbles and dreams of the French people. Their message was sometimes downright provocative, directed against the feudal lords, their exploitation, perjuring church and arbitrary monarchy. The movement from an old order to a new social order to one based on liberty, equality, and fraternité. However, still, these cries for change were heard against the lively beats and French folk music. The songs challenged defiant statements, imposed in strong, deft music structures. So the drum of the people played again, and called for action, the music of the French Revolution replayed.

The people's songs of the revolution weren't necessarily music written by professional musicians, or composed by them, but they were a part of the people's collective consciousness. The revolutionaries sang them in the streets; in the taverns; in the workshops; and in the field, singing about their various experiences and perspectives. Many times the songs were improvised or adapted from preexisting folk tunes embellished with new lyrics to suit an ever changing political landscape and an ever changing revolution. The revolutionary songs, for instance, were a spontaneous product as well as manifestations of an intense popular upsurge, and this spontaneous and collective nature of these songs underscored their authenticity and effectiveness in making their way in the air of masses and spreading feelings of solidarity, of a unified purpose, of a common front and sense of mass participation.

There is little question that the revolutionary songs' capacity to straddle social and regional divisions, turning disparate people of various occupations and locations into a common army of sorts, was one of their most remarkable qualities. Peasants and workers, soldiers and seamen, men and women, young and old sang the songs of the revolution. Wherever they were sung, in the city or country, north or south, east or west. These songs spoke to the nation's grievances and aspirations, united in their sentiments of class, region and occupation, and united in their sense of national unity and purpose.

The disseminating of information and the shaping of public opinion were no less part of the information transmission contributed by the revolutionary songs. Amid an age without mass media, the songs of the revolution became a way of passing information, convey ideas, and expressing sentiments throughout the entire country. Generally, the songs went in public gatherings, such as at markets, fairs and festivals, and so they could reach a larger audience. Besides, they were also printed in broadsheets and pamphlets, which were distributed to many people to read and those who could not read were read out. Socmed was, in some ways, a leading role in the writing of the narrative of the revolution as the songs became a key part of making the revolution.

The power of folk music as both a weapon and an organizer of resistance found in the French Revolution did not remain there, but was used in other revolts and rebellions around French history. A good example of this is the Vendée uprising of 1793 in the west of France, a counterrevolutionary rebellion. A variety of such factors contributed to the uprising of which the chief was the imposition of the Civil Constitution of the Clergy, which attempted to bring the Catholic Church under the control of the state, and the conscription of young men into the revolutionary army. Deeply religious, fiercely independent people, the Vendéeans rebelled against the revolutionary government because these measures were seen as an attack on their traditional way of life.

Tucked within a rich tapestry of folk songs that responded to the unique experiences, grievances, and aspirations of the Vendée uprising, the Vendée uprising was accompanied by a folk song blithe. The songs of the Vendée consisted of songs of a profoundly religious and royalist tendency, singing the rebels' loyalty to the Church and of the monarchy and their hatred of the revolutionary government. Frequently the blend of these songs' melodies invoked the rich centre of French folk music, with its vigorous rhythms and appealing tune, as a strong sonic backdrop for an equally strong counter-revolutionary message.

The song's powerful call to resistance and solidarity spoke to the people of the Vendée and it was quickly taken up by soldiers, peasants and priests as an anthem of the uprising, being sung by soldiers on the march into battle and on the streets at the call of protests. At once the enduring popularity and resonant power of folk music as a function of dissent, as a foundation for solidarity and as a driver of community in revolts and revolutions.

Like those of the French Revolution, the songs of the Vendée uprising were not purely entertainment, but effective protest, solidarity and mobilisation. They defined the providence of the days and had articulated the grievances of people and brought them around the cause of resistance and rebellion. In the streets, in the taverns, workshops, and fields the songs of the Vendée were sung, who varied the experiences and perspectives of the rebels. The songs were frequently improvised or indeed adapted from pre-existing folk tunes with new verses being interpolated to reflect the changing political context and new urgencies of the uprising itself. The songs of the Vendée were thus spontaneous and collective, authentically resonant and just the sort of tool for the mobilisation of the populace and the creation of a sense of shared purpose and solidarity that would help them fight one of the bloodiest wars ever to be fought on the soil of France.

That power of folk music to be a tool for protest, for mobilisation, for solidarity did not begin and end with the French Revolution and the Vendée uprising, but resounded in other uprisings and rebellions through French history. The songs of rebellion and resistance have been a staple of the fight for freedom and justice since the 14th century Jacquerie, a peasant revolt from northern France, through to the 19th century Paris Commune, a socialist uprising that rocked Paris. And these songs, with such powerful words of dissent, solidarity, mobilisation, reflect the spirit of the times, voice the people's bone of contention, nudge the people to haul up in the trench and stand for resistance and rebellion.

Additional crucial functions that the songs of rebellion and resistance have played in such means of transmission and transmission in cultural heritage and collective memory. These songs' melodies and lyrics have been kept alive through the generations, keeping stories, experiences and dreams of who was singing them.

Analyzing the ancient melodies and powerful lyrics of songs of the revolution and resistance gives us a window into the soul of a nation, a window into a nation's cultural heritage and a nation's people. Folk music as a method of protest, solidarity, and mobilization can be said to persevere in the musical heritage of the French Revolution, the Vendée uprising and other rebellions and uprisings through French history. Through songs of rebellion and resistance, the songs of struggle, hope, and the strength of the human spirit, they speak to a compelling story of our past and our present, of resistance and hope.

Modernization and Nationalism

France in 1799 when Napoleon Bonaparte took the chance and seized power was in a transitional state. Napoleon came and established stability and brought new laws internally and a new legal system of the Napoleonic structure. But he added more French empire territory to the European continent as well. Probably this period was marked by the development of national consciousness and identity in France. Partaking in French culture and society to one degree or another in different ways and to various degrees, Napoleon in large part created this identity in French culture and society knowingly or unwittingly. One of them was folk music which already in the first half of the nineteenth century actively joined the French people.

Before the period of Napoleon's coup d'état, France had not been stable, and did not receive direction and guidance after the French Revolution. French Revolution which culminated in the execution of Louis XVI, was followed by Reign of Terror under Robespierre followed by a plethora of government in a very short span of time, all this must have physically and mentally left French people tired and divided. The neighbouring relations and languages also dominated across the regions of the country. The folk songs of the peasants during this period mainly encompassed locality or complaint against one or the other obnoxious ruler or policy.

Many of them included local and regional languages, as well as informal languages that were unique to particular provinces. Nationalism was still relatively young and most of the rural provinces were not united.

When Napoleon took the reign he was very determined to get over this problem of instability most especially HIV/AIDS. In dealing with domestic affairs he set various policies to set law and order and ensure that presidential power is absolute. Events such as the code Napoleon (trying to standardize the French laws), centralising the bureaucratic structure and throughout the taxation policy performed major reforms. His ministry of public instruction in early years of revolutionary period brought education also on par throughout France. Such infrastructures as new roads and canals connected the provinces. Napoleon also occasionally had freedom of religion and press to achieve the support of common people. Most importantly he supported an ideology which dealt with the duty and loyalty to the state. Some of these policies were thought-provoking but Napoleon was able to do what was right after so much turmoil. These reforms integrated the French people in new forms to which common national identity that was in the process of formation could be linked.

He kept nationalism high by focussing on perpetual conquests and England's superiority over France.. As a representative of the French Revolution, Napoleon pronounced himself calling for liberty and bringing enlightenment to Europe by dint of enlarging France. Of all the arts during the renaissance, he mobilized painters, writers, poets, and musicians to celebrate his image and patriotism. In addition, propaganda paintings depicted Napoleon crossing the Alps in the same way that Hannibal crossed the alps, and presenting him as well as his armies similar to the great roman legionnaires. He staged performances of power such as the crowning himself Emperor in 1804 which used pagan images of Imperial Rome, Catholic motifs and Revolutionary emblems that all his people could relate to. In the context of the French Revolution Napoleon continued with construction of a personality cult though use of propaganda to create nationalist devotion to himself as the French state personified.

He was well aware culture and public opinion would come to Napoleon's aid, helping him to consolidate power and rule. During his leadership, artists and performing troupes were taken to the provinces to bring acceptable productions that educated the rural peasants regarding culturally accepted plays that praised Napoleon's victories. It simply shifted into this project of spreading propaganda to which folk music found itself roped into. In this case, the state paid for and provided 'state sponsored' folk singers to go around the countryside and perform songs that promoted Napoleon or his victories. This improved dissemination of relational topoi or emblems – success stories and heroes that one or more nations could employ to construct the foundation for unity.

Like the heroic Briton or the exemplary colonial, the Napoleonic image also glorified the French soldier, especially a noble farmer at war for his nation. This image also penetrated folk culture, as rather minimalistic songs telling about ordinary conscripts' heroic features, such as courage, honor or even sacrifice. These songs mourned young men who left their sweet hearts and homesteads to fight foreign aggressors bent on quashing revolutionary spirit. They glorified warfare as a crusade in the sake of "la patrie" which means home or country. Regardless of whether direct propaganda of this sort was effective or not, this cultural narrative elevated the peasantry while it also rallying the nation behind Napoleon who represents expansionism.

Other wartime folk songs of this period have turned into somber or melancholic notes. They concentrated on things lost and many of their stories were of villages conquered, crops spoiled because people were gone to war, wives weeping for their lost husbands and mothers mourning sons who died far away from home. These songs depicted the extent and the tragedy of warfare for civilians who were expected to endure immense pain for Napoleons continued wars away. Yet these sad tunes sometimes bore testimony to fidelity to the revolutionary cause, and in their faith in a just Frenchmen's fight.

In a way, Napoleon also made some unexpected contributions to French folk culture that further strengthened nascent themes of nationalism. Excessive taxation and the repeated mobilization of the young men from the peasant households exercised considerable social friction and opposition. And, indeed, due to the ruinous taxes or compulsory recruitment to military service, many fled their homes and became lawbreakers. There was also a similar culture to the story of legendary robbers and smugglers who battled corrupt officials and helped the people. All these bandit tales were present before the revolution, although they contrived up with considerably more proliferation. To local people, such as pecasants, some bandits of France were vindicated with being lawbreakers, but freedom fighters, who fought against the incoming culture that Napoleon was bringing to change.

Probably the most important cause was deep-rooted peasant injustices against the urban gentry as well as noble class which at times erupted to rebellion due to high taxes and scarcity of food. For example, propaganda in folk songs: Napoleon, the new tyrant — the reign of the panic King despite suffering peasants' need for bread like all other kings. Nevertheless, a majority of outlaw and protest songs remained in oral tradition within specified villages. These micro-level dissenting strains of national identity did not prevent the spread of French identity in macro level national cultures.

Last but not the least, this paper shows that Napoleon's endeavors in infrastructure development that led to integration of regional economies helped boost movement across different provinces. This allowed borrowing of musical and storytelling materials from one folk culture to another and the initial process of developing a French music type. Napoleonic reforms first opened up areas that where previously closed to once isolated rural communities. Ubiquity of transportation and markets that demanded more and more movement of people and shared media commonalities. Education that was standardized and the communication that was standardized provided people who were heterogeneous with set points of references to history. Gradually, over a few generations, these influences came together to portray a unifying folk culture as peasants of France conferred more musical & storytelling similarities. As regional vernaculars drifted to become versions of Parisian French, an amalgamate of peasant cultures became the basis from which a broadly available but culturally common base music was created and understood by the term popular music. Various norms of local naïveté contributed tastes within the stew of French folk song.

Marius Brotherson | Napoleon's Lasting Imprint on French Identity

Suffice it to say that Napoleon's imperial rule lasted for less than a decade. But in the course of the shifting timeline, he introduced rigorous centralized policies and propaganda while the long term cultural changes permanently overthrew the idea of national consciousness. Napoleon presented conceptions of French grandiosity that subsequent citizens could not but incorporate as objectively French. It developed into a legend that his self-presenting as the incarnation of the French nation. He provided citizenship to diverse people common reference points whether in real or in memory, or elements articulated in culture and or stories regardless of the region.

,but loss of so many French lives under Napoleon also helped in promoting national unity through people's loss and the trauma of the war. Years of fighting gave peoples time to mourn the many that died for « la patrie ». Despite this, the notion of Napoleonic culture as an entity born of great hardship would endure for many a generation later, in part because latter 19th century conflicts brought the Napoleonic image back into relevance as the cultural icon of patriotism.

In numerous more or less direct manners, Napoleon contributed to the construction of French culture in ways that helped form new feelings of national identity after the division of the revolutionary years. This interaction between Napoleonic ideological legacy and folk music can be traced in semiosis of several tracks that embodied and reproduced various aspects of Napoleon's impact in years that shaped what it might mean to be properly French. Napoleonic themes and reminiscence popular in France for many years after his reign as emperor. Napoleon's large-scale historical effect hence showed that significant cultural references and those common histories and narratives handpicked shaped a sustainable national consciousness from basic peasant folklore.

New and dramatic changes in France's socio-economic growth were shaped during the 19th century by the Industrial Revolution which shifted the country from the ranks of a primarily agricultural population to a complicated system of factories and large-scale production of goods. Such a sharp break from rural culture naturally brought about great changes to all aspects of the folk arts and music.

Folks songs have always been prominent in the life of provinces of France; they have been used for leisure purposes but also to meet certain needs. In rural villager's cultural events such as the folk songs and dances were important activities that acted as sources of unity and identity. Most songs served a function of keeping people in harmony and rhythm while working…planting, harvesting, spinning, weaving etc; religious song and dance were common factors in calendar customs and Catholic rites. Folk music was the only music which could be listened to before Industrial Revolution in France.

Such folkways of rural living were utterly uprooted by industrialization and urban shifts in the nineteenth century. Factory produced jobs drew millions from their ancestral small holdings to noisy conurbations such as Paris, Lyon, Lille, and Marseilles. The familiar social structures that had for mentions supported generations collapsed from its pressures of change. Oral tradition as passed from generation to generation became less effective once families were scattered and rural ways seemed increasingly out of place in cosmopolitan life.

At the same time, two processes that became dominant in French culture started reviving French folk music as other aspects of people's folk culture were decaying. Secondly, distinct fascination with a fast Records fading rural life increased interest in documenting songs and tales of rural France. Second, rural immigrants comprised new orchestras from the old folk styles to contemporary city life, thus catering for the new 'urban employees' kind!!!

Even before industrialization's effects became more significant, some enlightenment philosophers such as Rousseau depicted peasants as 'noble savages' whose lifestyles were better than the corrupting trends of the modernity they depicted. This image of a better pastky related to farming and agriculture was still further idealized during the storms of the 1800s. Growing and sophisticated urban consumers who were sometimes anxious by social transformation looked back for a harmonious rural idyll.

A proto-nationalist passion also came to value French material culture against neigbouring aggression – from the old-French nobility as well as the Anglo-American industrial invasion. Traditional squirism of province denoted the rudimentary feature of French national character, as far as Romanticism was a concern. This ideological movement oversaw great efforts to categorize, index, restore and promote the folk cultural tradition.

Prominent folklore researcher include Théodore Hersart de la Villemarqué, Jean-Jacquès Rousseau and Paul Sébillot who toured the French countryside of the 19th century with the elders to record lyrics and tunes. The ones published by the authors of the collections – for instance, Toussaint de la Villemarqué in his Gwerzioù Breizh-Izel of

1839 – imposed the consideration of folklore as a cultural phenomenon suitable for educated people and serving as a source of inspiration for enthusiasts. These scholars also gave numerous lectures to encourage people to take folk songs as a serious study, all while societies continued to modernize.

This scholarly impetus was supplemented in the performance arena where artists recaptured banned folks forms as part of the endorsement of nationalist traditionalism against emergent foreign pop influences. Among performing artists, Théodore Botrel, for example, singers of trios Les Trois Lucs, thus, activating the wave of interest in regional folk genres. Another province that was also reintroduced in oral tradition was folk dance originated from. In this way, folk music became more significant as one of the proved values of cultural memory as documented by various performance.

While the provincial folk forms were thus being frozen into commodifiable objects suitable for celebration, they were also adapting more creatively, from one point of view, to the circumstances of working class urban landscapes. Country people migrating to cities continued to bring their folk music aesthetics to urban areas and contextualizing Indigenous repertoires by integrating newly arriving instruments, rhythms, and lyrics that captured industrial existence.

Already the cabarets and dance halls of urban centres became places of multiple ethnicity confluence where this process generated new, dynamically developing syncretic song repertoires, which were popular across the regional and class divides. People of the working class engaged themselves dancing on Viennese waltzes, Scottish reels, Italian tarantellas and even folk movements enlivened by modern tunes at the Bal Bullier dance hall. Musette, dance music of Auvergne and migrants from Limousin with banjo replaced the Paris Café musical floor.

Likewise, the subject matter of the songs in folk mused moved from the simple village life. Songs described the oppression in factories or offered a glimpse of the luxurious life in the emerging megalopolis, adding socially realistic elements to folk idioms. Trips to prisoners or penal settlements produced such chain gang songs as Le Temps des Cerises, whose tunes were tailored for synchronous work. However, working-class folk music also sang of pleasures of love, ale, dancing and insolent freedom in the cocktail of the city. This "muse populaire" enabled rural folk media to speak for the new audience of the newly-formed urban proletariat.

However, some bourgeois scholars regarded these popular mutations as low imitative impairments and vulgarised versions with no refinement of the classic provincial folklorized norms. However, many artists and activists focused on the tenacity, creativity and defiance of immigrant musicians in the streets, and in the cabarets. As minstrels of the Middle Ages, these popular entertainers aimed at making new cultural bridges that would fit a fast evolving age.

That tension between static reconstructions of an idyllic rural folk life and dynamic hybridization into complex urban forms persisted well into the latter half of the twentieth and beyond. However, throughout the 1930's many communists and slow agrarian political groups deliberately exploited regional dance and instrumental styles that appealed to the lowly working populace. Its political aspect is traced to the Vichy regime and occupation when Cathars singers sang French resistance in disguised folk songs.

The early post war years brought cosmopolitan folky fusion that married African American jazz, Algerian rai, gypsy swing, Brazillian samba and bal musette or java French accordion dance pop. Some influential musicians, such as Sidney Bechet or Django Reinhardt, brought the refined element of the sophistication of the lineage of folk music though the Authentic folk culture of the villages was fading. However the 1960s saw the French youth as active consumers, in English and American rock-n-roll's rebellion; a

French equivalent chanson revival in the search of authenticité took inspiration from medieval French instead of foreign rhythm.

However, the modern world persistently extends its influence on manifestations of traditional culture. New media technologies of digital distribution and globalization of popular music industries enable access to rural folk archives at the same time as that to contemporary world musics. The isolation of Old Regime France that permitted distinctly French oikos dialects has been disrupted by mass communication; nevertheless regional revivals like Breton's Sonerien Du do not accept globalization homogenization by consciously stressing language and instruments giving them a pointedly "Other" status.

Parallel dynamics thus currently occur across almost all the cultures, which are in a process of both discontinuity from the original origins and of emerging new creative opportunities. The lamps of traditions go on to enlighten human truths that no longer have support at their birthplaces.

At the start of the first half of the 19th century, the French nation was only gradually groaning under the burden of nationalism. In the last decade of the 18th century the French revolution overthrew the monarchy and formulated conceptions of liberté, égalité, fraternité – liberty, equality, and brotherhood. A new kind of Frenchness formed on Republican principles rather than on the devotion to a monarch.

There was a rise of French nationalism in the early 1800 when Napoleon was on conquest to conquer Europe with pride in the French army. But defeat in the 1815 France and restoration of monarchy opposed the early nationalism. For the remaining part of the 1800s France tried to stabilize its political system; however, it went through the cycle of monarchy, republic, and empire. This political turmoil actually fueled French nationalism because people embraced French ethos and identity all the more.

This volatile 19th century French folk music asserted nationalism and understood to act as a source of defiance. A lot of this folk music was descended from peasants that inhabited the French countryside for several generations, which was the French people and their language as well as customs put into song. These folk songs were about history of

France, its geography, love and misfortune – it was people's history after all.

Others also drew regional emotions, using regional diction and music styles. Some regional idioms mentioned are musique normande from Normandy, musette and bourree from Auvergne and Lyonnais, Occitan music from the southern France. Some of these regional styles exists even to this present day as part of France musical culture.

During the Franco-Prussian War (1870-71), folks songs sung about previous French victories against the Germans. Choruses were to inform the citizens they hold such responsibility to protect the French nation.

Before the First World War, such radical tunes as 'Liberté ou la mort!' of 'La Marseillaise' (in use since 1792) emerged again in calling the citizens to arms. Other folk songs also rose in this period such as the regional songs where local volunteer regiment marched into war singing regional tunes.

Opposition as well as revolutionary workers and radicals sang about and against politics in many political dissatisfied periods or during revolution; for instance, during the formation of Paris Commune in 1871. Songs continued to protest against injustice within working poor French people.

Consequently, folk music enabled the different classes and peoples in France to speak loudly of nationalism during the war and political turmoil. They sang songs, spoke and sang the language, and even sang tunes that were common to both the high-status, huge-city slicker, and the lowly, rural hick; all of which made them feel more linked as French citizens.

Lakmé, Opus 31, an opera written in 1881 by Léo Delibes with music by Leo Delibes, introduced Breton melodies into musical culture — but this takes place under colonialism in India. In the Bacchanale dance scene of Act II, we find Breton bagpipes and bombards, used in a vigorous music scene, in the defence for themselves by the Breten people against British colonial troops. The message was clear – folk culture as the French nationalism resistance against external enemies.

Next were modality and staccato rond rhythm characteristic of French folklore, – The pieces of piano as Miroirs (1905) and Gaspard de la nuit (1908). This made his music.to have a national character that intentionally avoided the hegemonic Germanic symphonic trends.

They also used another rising trend of interest toward the French folks' traditions to create the French national musical culture during this time by such distinguished composers. The new French pieces they were writing and performing belonged to the fleetingly popular classical tradition which spoke to the growing nationalism prevalent in the bourgeoisie class.

Nonetheless, regional folk music experienced a slow erosion throughout late 19th/early 20th century France. When transportation was developed, many people from countryside also moved to cities for job opportunities. They also grew also the urban popular culture in terms of cabarets and mass media including radio. Thus, rather distinguishable regional variants fused into more uniform national folk or parade-ground strains.

The bloodshed of World War I also destroyed a generation who grew up with local peasant songs. People who escaped carnage were left with no way of dealing with dreadful experiences that linked to familiar tunes played during the occasion. As much as nationalism remained an important force, the local processes that contributed to it were being decimated.

Initially, by 1920, the cultural protectors of the French music feared that unique folk music species of regional identities were fast fading away. Breton, Basque and Occitan, with others, were fading off or forbidden from schools. The problems were solved with the formation of the National League for the Defence of Regional Language and Folklore in 1925.

Before they vanished from the countryside, there were collectors for other record labels such as Pathé and Columbia to send collectors in to get folk songs. Live performances are also used to record present music tones for future research as current tones are not the same as way back.

State Radio France launched national folk groups such as the International Institute of Comparative Music Studies and Documentation in 1944, whose function was to record and perform folk music.

Large collections of public folk songs were gathered just as, Julien Tiersot's French Popular Songs which is the 3 part collection of melodies and lyrics from the years 1887 to 1889.

Thus, by the middle of the twentieth century, French cultroma was conscious of the utility of folk tune study to taelpate nationality – and endeavoured so future generations might also have the opportimity of rediscovering their individualistic regional identity in the larger perceptions of nationalist tradition.

Thus, despite homogenization and globalization trends, which move further into the 21st century, French folk melodies retain indisputable images of nationalisms. Even these minstrel-popularized modals such as 'frère jayque' are sung to date as national progeny heart to heart repeatedly. Bombardes and biniou flutes, still also conduct fest-noz dances which are from Brittany and are centuries in age and very much in evidence at festivals. While fewer in number, regionalisms such as those found in Alsace, Corsica, and Auvergne continue to fight the assimilation from something national.

The French football team mobilizes the nation for international competition then and only then the folk tunes intermingle with the chants, anthems, and fight songs. Hence, though politics splits the population in the present society, folk excited the national pride that holds the French population together. It is about the persistence of the link between folk melodies and French identity from the age of

19th century proto nationalism to 1990s pop culture.

20th Century

In the late 1950s and early 1960s French Youth became increasingly dissatisfied with the conservative and consumerist French popular culture. These did lay the ground work for a revival of French folk music as part and parcel of other occurring countercultural trends associated with the cult of peace, love, and live in harmony with the nature. School children in france started searching for their roots as a true French person by tracing back to old French folks and their instruments of music. This French folk revival would go on liberating the depth of French folk tradition to those who would come later.

Le développement du folk français a pu être accompagne de la montée des stars folk-rock Americane ou Anglo-Saxonne telle que Bob Dylan ou Joan Baez dès 1960. This roots oriented vocals and strings style, and its relationship to the political left and counter culture living began to found traction with French youth. This made many young French people look at the folk tradition of regions such as Brittany, Corsica and Occitanie previously dismissed for generations as simply old fashion peasant music.

It also spoke of a desire for dusty humanistic tones than the frail intricate orchestral styles composed by establishment musicians of the time. The use of folk instruments such as the hurdy-gurdy, bagpipe, accordion and the violin helped to get the aspect of the national folk tradition as well as the rustic village life before civilization by advanced technology. Youth attitudes of romantic revolutionism 'getting back to the garden', 'the liberty to dream', 'civil disobedience', 'coming of age' May 1968, revolution, protests, terrorism, anarchy were inspired by political events such as civil unrest of May '68.

The area of the Breton peninsula with the rather Italo-Celtic grounded folklore and ethnographic background became the focus of fedhood folklore revival by the late 1960s. Breton folk music had endured similar challenges for centuries, even though the lifestyle of Britons had been actively suppressed by the French crown. Thus, trios Breton folk rock of a new generation like Tri Yann, Sonerien Du and Kornog started gaining national fame for their electrification of traditional Breton dansant / shanty songs and for composing new Breton lyrics folk-rock music.

Following the release in 1970 of an album simply entitled Reflets, Alan Stivell begins the tour around the world that will establish him as the mythical figurehead of a Celtic folk movement celebrated everywhere. Stivell's reindigenization process of traditional Breton harp music along with rock guitar and drums in songs such as 'Pop Plinn', helped open global ears and reflexivity to localized folk resources for young musicians. The large public concerts, which took place at the Olympia theatre and the spectacle of following Stivell introducing Breton folk music to France on national television ensured a following that proclaimed the Breton as the French folkmusic renaissance.

In the other districts of France such as in Paris, there was another style sometimes categorised as New French Song singer-songwriter style by the early 1970s—the other side of the French folk revival.. Léo Ferré, Georges Brassens, Claude Nougaro, Jean Ferrat and Serge Reggiani created poetic realist chansons and ballads putting France poetry and literature to use for their acoustic folk songs. These musician-poets developed a persona of steward of liberty and held their public spaces – street corner and cabaret – to the standard of their earliest inspirations, the medieval troubadours.

La chanson francaise was not an exclusively band-driven phenomenon: the lyrical bent toward idealism, matched with a musical aesthetic supposedly influenced by Breton peasant instruments, aligned these performers to the cause of folk-minded collectives. Together they broadened French folk identity away from traditional dance rhythms to literary feelings based on appreciation for the ground and the human person's equal worth across the divide of class. They made up the normative substance of a counterculture that was in the process of formation.

The revival developed into a movement across France over the period of 1970-1976 through circuits of new Folk music festivals specifically for French regional artists as a reaction to rock music. The analyzed festivals, Festivals Interceltiques de Lorient in Brittany, Festival de Musique et Traditions Populaires Méditerranéennes de Marseille, and Festival de la Musique et de la Danse Traditionnelle de Chateauroux, valued a non-electric approach, communalism, and the unity of the nation/ world through local heritage. These functions provided the geographically scattered regional Frenchfolk-art personages with a means by which to find common cause with each other and transmuted numerous rock aficionados into a richer, earthsharer 'authentic' brand of French folk artistry.

The natural organic grow French folk scene contributed this folk festival circuit and Malicorne, Gabriel Yacoub, Pierre Bensusan, Dan Ar Bras, and La Souleuvre artists which experimented accoustic French folk fusion opportunities. In this period the music moved from revivalists to contemporary interpreters of a tradition and not imitations of it. From mid 1970s, the French folk revival was a healthy living folk artists' community who pursue folk identity, instrument and vocal style, and spirituality which harmonize the global folk currents as well as nurturing the soul of French soil.

Some of the instruments that came from the backstage and became famous with the help of the French folk revival are such as hurdy-gurdy; it is a rather old stringed instrument in the shape of an arch, which is performed with the help of turning the wheel covered in rosin with special crank; this crank touches the strings and thereby creates rather special drones. Until Stivell, Yacoub, Malicorne and Ar bras emerged to give the instrument a new rich style of concert-ready hurdy gurdy that fit ensemble playing and a new fiddle and rippling drone guitar and percussion sound.

This hurdy gurdy revival was based on Breton and Centrals French styles and materials, in addition to new instrumentals for hurdy gurdy from the album and songs with medieval feelings. Musique Cevenole, the last hurdy gurdy maker, which witnessed an increased demand as a result of the French folk revival of the 1970's, began designing the new light-built concert models with guitar-type machine heads for tuning certainty. Quickly, new French hurdy gurdies were being purchased all across Europe and the Americas as enthusiasm towards the envelope across the folk scene internationally intensified. The hurdy gurdy music therefore evolved into symbolizing the ability to move past history and place conventions epitomized by the folk instruments related with timeless mythical past and pilgrimage.

Thus, the French folk revival posed as a mediator which conveyed prospective international and spiritual trends of 1970s popular music. Folk-rock music by Breton harpist Alan Stivell, influenced Irish bands like Planxty that started Ireland's folk revival and in the 1980 & 90s sped up a craze of Celtic traditional music all around the globe. On East West stylistic syntheses, it also precedes the World Music movement and contributed to the acculturation of French and Celtic folk in the New Age music.

At the same time the folk festivals circuit was offering a supportive context where American folk legends such as Bob Dylan, Joan Baez and Mimi Farina shared stage with French troubadours or folk ensembles in the name of the folk music heritage that provided an antidote to the commercialization of popular culture. This mutual exchange fanned folk revivals throughout the studied zone of the Atlantic world. When important rock musicians like Paul Simon, Peter Gabriel and others launched the World Music movement at the end of the 1980s, in France the folk revival influenced the formation of the context for a global discussion of local music as the representation of universal human identity.

The great irony of the French folk revival lie in the fact that sounds which once alluded to a desire to escape modernity are now widely acknowledged architectural features of modern French identity. Breton-Celtic harp of Alan Stivell, pounding bombard drums, churning hurdy gurdy of the bourrée dance tunes of the Centre France, Occitan tongued airy female vocals such as those of Clàudia Caneit all have returned to France from cultural periphery as authentic Gallic moods and as the new shade of Frenchness for the World of the New France.

Starting from the young people's idealized search for realness of countryfolk, it evolved into the contemporary serial re-ethnicisation of

French culture – a mnemonic touchstone for millennial youth who have lost soul in consumerism, a call back to historical roots and values. The folk revival helped to feed modern styles of various styles such as French indie rock, Celtic new age, medieval folk for music, French rap, and French world fusion music that incorporate acoustic folk at will without worry over the incongruity or retro-revival. It was therefore in calling up the spirits of pre-modern France that the French folk revival let them loose on the present. These decentralizations from ancient forests and bonfire circle dances remain superimposed on the skin of postmodern French culture and reiterated in synergy with the digital nets of the Francophone country.

French folk music has tradition which includes the prehistoric folk music and the folk music which is from all regions of the country. The music of Brittany gives the energetic performances from folk instruments that represent France at present or the poetic songs of Occitania from France have also described a number of folk genres in France. But in recent decades these folk idioms have also began to impact modern trends as performers include regional motifs into fresh hybrids and electronics experiments. The heavy example is felt strongly in Electridance music and world fusion where French elements of folk music have made a strong entry. This proves a collection of remarkable combinations of tradition and contemporary design.

A fest noz is a celebration originally linked to Breton dance events, and this particular genre has given birth to several electronic derivatives where the acoustic instruments like the bagpipe and hurdy-gurdy meet synthetic pads and dance rhythms. Concerning Breton music further, bands such as Deep Forest experimenting in world-beat dance mechanism have used vocal and melodies from Breton songs. The buzzing bagad pipe bands are also remixed adding blood-pumping EDM hits and the crispiness of the biniou into new versions. In fact, producers use even the perfect songs of the old Kan ha diskan singers reverb by playing nice parts of the recordings within noisy ambient soundscapes. While they become transmitted via modern technologies, these are symbolic of regional roots. Their attitude also works the other way around however, nowadays some younger Breton folks revivalists like Clarisse Lavanant sings traditional repertoire over electronic beat or "dub" production. The synergies show that mature vernacular traditions can be powerful sources of ideas for hybrid forms.

Occitania, the southern part of France has also influenced contemporary fusions of folk culture. The versify and sinuous melodies are the integral part of Troubadour's lyrics, accompanied by typically Occitan instruments such as a fiddle and pipes and the vielle à roue or the hurdy-gurdy. Some of the current younger Occitan folk groups like Fabulous Trobadors, Massilia Sound System and La Talvera use these traditional elements combined with rock, reggae and pop making 'products' that should appeal to the current market. It recalls the figurative and creative way of writing Occitan song through these renditions in particular, for the great singers such as Claude Marti. The same can be said with the electric hurdy-gurdy performed by Valentin Clastrier of La Talvera. Here, French-Arabic group Watcha Clan go even further, mixing samples of Occitan folk singers with

Moroccan Chaabi, Gnawa and electro-Maghrebi dance flour. These experiments afford opportunities for Occitan music to become integrated into new global subjectivities in a manner where issues of linguistic and lyrical endowment remain magnificently relevant. These deeper roots growing from the troubadour tradition bear new fruits as a result of modern contact.

The provincial mountain zones of France centuries contain exceptional kinds of acid folk guitar pertaining to agrestic occupied populations. Traditions from Auvergne and Savoie have become especially introduced to relax and ambient electronica in recent years thanks to perceived nature recordings by Ocora label. Reverberant vocal resonations, soprano and/or tenor piercings, produced by the traditional alpine choirs are resampled to electronic spaces by producers such as

Pheek and Deejay Punk-Roc to recreate a meditative serenity. Also contemporary composers of Neoclassical such as Bruno Mantovani also uses the raw sound of the rugged hurdy-gurdy and vocal cries of the Savoyard music in its electroacoustics, as a referent to memory. Other artists of electronica use old shepherds' calls and mountain tunes recorded on old disc as rhythm section, turn them into hooks for loops. Live recordings of rural music events of Auvergnat performed by the French sound artist Bernard Fort are also integrated with sonar minimal techno forays. These textures metaphorically ground these electronic fusions back into a rural French idyll, conjuring folkloric memories from its Alpine valleys even when it is reimagining them across synthetic ones.

In Louisiana, a distinctive branch of the French-speaking folk music tradition is alive and well, their special party flavor being fiddling and Caucasian dance music in the jelly roll accordion key. As Cajun music has evolved and merged overseas it has returned to infuse French electronica through probes and virtual guest spots. Such labels as Natch Records engage Cajun music seeking fiddle melodies, Voiries shouting and dancing beats in the archival field recordings to turn them into modern dance instrumentals. Other bands do trad-Cajun; and zydeco with funky electronica elements—Saints Go Marching are one such group. The given 20 years anniversary compilation of the Toulouse-based Bacchanal label included even a virtual interaction between Cajun accordionist Joel Savoy and French turntablist DJ Slow based on the Cajun accordion samples – with disco edits. These pan atlantic exchanges provide symbolic links through the language and enable the Cajun culture to sound in new places. Additionally it is worth mentioning that many such as the Nouvelle Orleans festival which paints their Bourbon Street show presented yet additional possibilities for french and Cajun performers to meet.

The cultural orientation of the Pied Noir community who migrated from Algeria now in France, has etched an indelible legacy of North African Jewish and Arabic musical memories to French popular music. The Orivas Y Achour groups and old singer named Salim Halali were famous through the Pied-Noir club circuit which paved way for more crossovers. Following the heritage of the above listed artists, more recent franco-Algerian productions, such as Gnawa Diffusion, Watcha Clan, Françoise Atlan, and Mehdi Haddab incorporate Maghrebian Arabic, Andalusian orchestral style with elements of punk-rock electronica style. The actual possibilities are quite vast; the very promising Egyptian-Lebanese band Imarhan incorporated French-Tunisian electronic producer Islam Chipsy recently, replacing their usual desert rock guitars with Chipsy's rhythmic synth beats. Such hybrids extend the homepage of North African music around the Mediterranean and incorporate it into new globalized subject formation. On this count, the Pied-Noir memory then sows other occasions even as it mourns lost ground.

The regions of Basque situating in both French and Spanish territories are also attributed to have deposited significant streams of impact into French fission genres because of their geographical liminal position. This has been particularly the case in the north of the Basque provinces in a region known as Gascony. Bernard Lubat became a stimulating musician of this avant-jazz groups who has been the earliest taking into consideration basque xirula flute and alboka reedpipe from the 1970s. Other groups that have branched off again, such as Kalakan, have expanded on the path he has laid out, using flamenco and Afro-Caribbean styles as well as producing exciting rhythmic appeglia. The Elirbo, other hybrid classical endeavors from the area, also write new pieces from older Basque melodies adapted to modern orchestral standards. These borderland sounds harness the possibilities of the in-between of Basque identity to create new formative areas of cross-over where traditions might meet organically across a roots/routes divide. This symbolic reterritorialisation of heritage here unfolds not through the straitened formalism of a pure and fixed heritage, but through the vocal liquidity of exchange creativity.

Other such works, such as Mass polyphonies like the paghjella, were originally products of medieval Christian religious confraternities or fraternities and were not expected to be part of the active canon. However visionary musicians have also managed to bring about new turns to their styles through fusion complexes. Singer Petru Guelfucci took this rout from 1970s onwards and used the haunting paghjella tune in contemporary psych-rock mode on albums such as Corsica. Younger artists such as the female vocal group of Corsican singers Voce di Corsica or the innovative sopranist Michèle Bernardi have also developed obviously experimental tendencies that might also appeal to the younger generation. For example Frenchzen and others have accepted polyphonic samples in the global mainstream electronica music to show that the samples are accepted. These antique resonance here, resonate the postmodern put up spaces, recalling to those who have forgotten pasts here, with newly heard.

Preservation and Globalization

There is probably no other European country that could boast so many regional folk songs and dances which were so varied owing to the great differences in the geographical nature of the country and the people. Starting from the waved farmlands of the Centre-Val de Loire region to the wilky shores of the Brittany, all the regions advanced arts and culture as the heritages of the soil, tongue and earning of people. Across the generations these vernacular forms encapsulated the nation within performance within song, communal feasting, and relevant celebrations and seasons respectively.

But, in the recent past, the forces of globalization and modernization are endangering many of these living heritage practices. Whereas young people increasingly choose to seek their livelihoods in cities and mass culture, small towns and villages suffer a shortage of inhabitants – and traditional performers. On the one hand, the young French generation is growing up in the world connected by the internet, and they influence such foreign music types as rock, hip-hop and electronic dance music. If specific action is not taken, extensive repertoires typical for rich regions will not be played any more.

As a result, grassroots organizations alongside the French government have employed a number of tactics to support endangered practices. They know about intangible culture as a component of the diversity and social coherence as well as the human well-being. If change always remains an inalienable constant of cultural evolution, the basic ideas of tradition, nevertheless, can be transmitted to the next generation. The following interventions help to demonstrate ideas for stability within change.

Since the 1970s and 1980s, folklorists and ethnomusicologists have been travelling around France to record musical genres in urban cities and countryside farmsteads. They collect sound archives, transcriptions, photographs, videos, CDs, DVDs, and informal interviews before couch potato styles and familiar sets erode. These field materials provide clear descriptions of traditions that might only exist at the research sites in archives at some future time.

More specifically, several important institutions are required to protect these threatened fragments. Through its extensive world-wide field recording projects the two Maison des Cultures du Monde centres in Vitré and Lorient have built significant collections. The Vatican's collection of religious music includes peasant songs of Catholic rural cult in southeastern France, archived in Sainte-Marie d'Ozon.

Some other organizations, however, act more as curators of collections. The Center for Traditional Music and Dance of Upper Brittany collects documentation but also funds new instruction, performances, and performance inspired by creative interpretation of the archive source. Their work maintains old songs and dances relevant within the area's living, growing culture. This way, a practice can be handed down through generation succession of tradition-bearers, and it would continue even if certain elder tradition-bearers have died.

However, apart from these grassroots initiatives, the French government has extended supporting plans at communal, area and country stage. Cultural institutions, which formerly concentrated on tangible heritage inclusive of monuments and museum, have embraced other endogenous cultural immaterial experience by equal measure important to national heritage. The Ministry of Culture now helps the masters of folk arts in regions to transfer the skills and not suffer financially. Certain cities have had special zoning and provisions related to traditional artisans who are so crucial for the city's image.

The largest of these developments was UNESCO's 2003 Convention for the Safeguarding of Intangible Cultural Heritage which stimulated the creation of new domestic efforts to preserve endangered traditions in the age of globalization. Today France has sound programs to identify and safeguard significant heritage: in 2006 it ratified the agreement. Some splendid singing and dancing cultures – the rhapsodic ballads of Occitania to the enthusiastic festivities of upper Brittany – have already been included in the list to draw public attention.

This increasing trend recognizes cultures as process-oriented and not a product or a set of artifacts that need to be protected by practice as much as they can be by storing or preservation. Hence, current social policies are to maintain living spirit rather than merely gather relics of a dying generation. They sanction situations where traditional arts may carry on to progress as living options in the palette of worlds cultura.

While archivists and policymakers are effecting strategies to support the continuation of folk arts within provinces of the country, tradition in France persists to be reshaped by globalization. At some point or another, younger musicians are able to incorporate external influences with core values when creating their musical standpoint. The result is new progressive folk genres that transposes the old songs into present reality.

This capability is most symbolized by singers such as Nolwenn Leroy, who are in the middle of provincial conservatism on one half and global modernity on the other. Though born in another part of France –particularly in a local of western Brittany–Leroy was bred in an Irish immigrant family savouring the Gaelic language and song, particularly the Celtic music. However, her pop albums in two languages are also liked by the youth across France and other parts of the world. Blending a more multicultural approach of folk tunes with the then pop instruments and electronic dance music to make heritage palatable to the contemporary generation.

Lo'jo is a band that combines even more distant worlds in fusions pieces. Over the years, this collective from Anjou has traveled through the Sahara to record with Tuareg musicians from Mali, blending punk guitars with dance rhythms and desert blues. Their boastful use of African aesthetic demonstrates how once isolated folk arts can grow through globalisation.

Based on Carroll's thesis, Young bands such as La Phaze and Da Break can also be identified as Pan-European. Ingredients are Celtic influences merged with Gypsy jazz, French song, North African Rai, and Jamaican reggae, and it is impossible to better categorize the music that they play. These are not provincial bands intending to preserve something older but international musicians who adapt traditions for the novel conditions.

This interlinkage of global influences is taken to a new level of integration by increased world music festivals such as Les Transmusicales, Les Vieilles Charrues and

Festival de Lorient. Intended for booking ethnically various folk and modern musicians from different countries of the periphery, these events develop love for local talents along with renowned foreign performers. For local bands, it is a chance to perform village-derived music in front of literally thousands of receptive young people. Audience expands and so as the influencing factors.

While preservation endeavors are a noble cause to save provincial music from eradications by global forces, traditional arts continue to endure because they evolve. Contemporary versions bring new ideas into maintenance and advancement of heritage without breaking that connection. As in this continuity, pertinence is ensured.

Collectors and archivists do a service by capturing the easily extinguished candle flames of marginal community activities. But, nevertheless, intangible culture exists, and perhaps even more than tangible culture, it exists through practice. However detailed, the records themselves contain no spark of the traditional meetings throbbing with spirit. The continued existence of these practices, first of all, depends on their transfer to interested heirs.

Here the effort goes beyond teaching relics of a fading culture This is a sharp contrast to the usual way of portraying other dying cultures as Studs Terkel himself points out. It means cultivating practices in which value is seen in arts that are relevant to people in today's society, that provide value to their socially constructed selves. This requires at the same time some type of innovative and growth along with the conservation. By adaptation, forms stay important across different generations.

Computerization always increases change to all manners of folkways with multiculturalism being the most common fall guy. But distinctions between tradition and modernity are somewhat blurred. The collectors attempt to prevent breaking of the pasts that are fading out, but the culture itself evolves out of new forms. Leroy, or Lo'Jo bear a lot of influences but they translate them through the spirit of their initiation to make of a sung style an inheritance contemporary and universal. In these encrypted forms the strata of the deep past continues to propagate into the emerging present.

Thus brings us to the policy of conservation without constraint and change without severance. Thus flexibility might have the basis of intangible heritage perhaps carry on meeting the contemporary requirement and more importantly seek the person to pursue the value in the future. Thus, the measures for protection also generate processes of rebuild and power as persons and places.

The represented practices, policies, and artists have remained the sources for the recording of the possibilities to keep going with progress during a period of transformation. Thus, in the light of archives and accessibility, classified local class and international arena; rural origin can possibly cultivate progressive identities. Tradition is much more a function of active engagement than it is a function of preservation. Passionate communities who continue to perpetuate these forms as the purpose that defines arts of a particular age, traditional arts of today are living cultures.

The Future

For some time, the French 'Chanson' which is rooted in French folk music identities, stories and very deep narratives has been of import for the French. Breton sailors' sad songs to Occitan dance music: These are continuing styles that have properly developed descendants, and have been collected, altered, and maintained for years by enthusiasts. There is however some solace for French folk artists because similar folk genre all over the world have found it hard to get young talent since the dominance of pop music and despite the grim picture Kurien paints about the future of French folk, there is some hope.

The folk revival scene has gained new momentum in recent years due to great festivals which reunited the best representatives of the folk scene with newcomers. Credited festivals such as the Festival Interceltique de Lorient attended by over 700000 people every August acts as a baseline for participation. The Festival of the Nights of Fourvière, a two months annual festival in arts that takes place every summer in the roman theatres of Lyon offers year after year an ambitious folk performers with differing cultures allowing new public to discover traditional music. That such festivals still feed off an audience speaks well for the potential of French folk to be large and good for many decades, as well as the next years.

Among the older generation of Breton musicians were Yann Tiersen, Sylvain Dufour, and Lizzy Mercier descloux and Nolwenn Leroy whose work blends traditional Breton music with a great deal of elements from modern pop culture. Though primarily composing soundtracks for movies and television, Tiersen admits his Breton culture in spaciously romantic music that has enthralled listeners globally. Dufour is an accordionist who puts different contemporary electronic spin into the dance-like music style of central France known as "Bistrot Electro" in jest. Brittany-born Leroy who was a contestant at 'Star Academy,' singing reality song competition show sings such intensely romantic songs originating from her region and has sold millions of recordings. These musicians give but a few examples of the future possible developments of French folk music.

Other platforms have also come with convenient new means through which other persons outside the culture can be exposed to French folk music. Field recordings and regional performances are no longer hidden treasures which require motivated individuals to search for vinyl LPs. With the help of Discover weekly and Release Radar, Apple Music and Spotify have the extensive French folk playlists containing recommendations for the potential audience at their disposal While sites such as YouTube and Facebook serve as the direct link to the folk sessions, concerts, and song tutorials at hand. Such extensive website visibility sets the stage for future expansion.

Technological development also opens the possibility for French folk musicians today also to infuse those elements that would have been impractical to include in live performance before. Contemporary drum machines, loop-station pedals, sampling keyboards, beat boxes, synthesizers etc are now able to provide the means for integrating new sonic timbres and/or grooves to the timeless soul. While listeners with their acoustic purity may argue electronic alterations and additions to the traditionally French sounds, the growing talents continue to efficiently weave technology to create suspense and interest throughout their performances withoutgetCrap lose of soul or passion.

Of course, French folk faces the serious danger of dying out if elder tradition-bearers and native language speakers fail, not to pass on their knowledge of such things as rare regional dialects, little performances, and performance techniques which involve instrument handling to the young ones. However, those offered by Kendalc'h, Sonerion, and other proper preservation societies are already fighting this reality to the bitter end with young artistic apprentices meeting their folk hero inspirations across France.

Though there is a strong and developing academic backing emerging progressively among ethnomusicologists globally, students, scholars, documenters, archivers and teachers of music from traditional genres to raise awareness all over the world. Books, journals and multimedia databases act as ready entry points to the relatively neglected French community dances, folk arts and dances, dances and a particular region's instruments for those who wish to actively engage in folk traditions. Modern university students even have the opportunity to earn a degree in the work of French folk songs and dances, choreography, ethnography, etc., as the subject further develops.

Such basic and time-honored folk genres as veillées [community song sessions], pardons [religious and folk pilgrimages], and rustic bals folk [nonprofessional country dances] may not have supporters as numerous or as highly energized as pop music concert-goers or today's "consultants" virtual hits; however, the living emotions are not small. The essential message of the French folk music always retain its relevance among the society. So long as that bond is maintained and appreciated French folk styles should continue to deservedly occupy their station in the nations cultural landscape in the future.

By the joined efforts of such devoted performers, helpful lends and saving technologies French folk music seems to be not only to continue to exist in the next decades, but to potentially bloom up. It may ultimately boil down to the following question: can global audiences, weaned on high production value commercial sounds, entertain the concept of homespun traditions of real people's songs? However, with up and coming young folk bands such as Duo de Twingo, Sirba Octet and Taÿfa one can see creative potential awaiting on the horizon. And benchmark artists across France perpetually compete at maintaining high standards and indeed pass inspiration down to the next generation.

Thus, according to the master musician and icon, Alan Stivell, it will be possible to know the ancient music of tomorrow through what remain today. If the past years are anything to go by then people across the globe can look forward to enjoying new directions in the French folk music as new generations from strong base branches new leaves towards future heavens.

Disclaimer

Everything shared in this book should be considered as educational and informative in nature. The author and publisher shall not be responsible for any loss or damage suffered by any reader directly or indirectly through reading of, reliance on, and use of information that only the author and the publisher know at the time of writing this book.

Some of the suggestions given and the approaches recommended in the book may not be applicable to certain circumstances. The author and the publisher shall not be held responsible for any damages caused as a direct result of the use or non-use of the information presented in this book.

It is understood that readers should not rely on it for professional solicitations such as medical, legal, financial, and other related opinions. If any professional help is needed, then advice of a competent professional person should be taken.

The author and the publisher will not be held responsible for direct, indirect, special, or consequential damages or any other costs whatsoever arising from the use of the information present herein in this book.

About the Author

Maher Asaad Baker (In Arabic: ماهر أسعد بكر), is a Syrian musician, author, journalist, VFX & graphic artist, and director. He was born in Damascus in 1977. He grew up with a dream of being one of the most well-known artists in the world, and he has been working hard to achieve it ever since.

He started his career in 1997 when he was only 20 years old. He had a passion for technology and media, and he taught himself how to develop applications and websites. He also explored various types of media-creating paths, such as music production, graphic design, video editing, animation, and filmmaking. He was not satisfied with just being a consumer of media; he wanted to be a creator of media.

Reading was another source of inspiration for him. He was always surrounded by books as a child, thanks to his father's extensive library. He read books from different genres, topics, and perspectives. He read books for knowledge, for wisdom, for entertainment, for enlightenment. Reading stimulated his imagination and curiosity. Reading also developed his writing skills.

He did not start writing professionally until later in his life, as he was busy with other projects and pursuits. But when he did start writing, he proved himself to be a talented and prolific writer. He wrote articles for various newspapers and magazines on topics such as politics, culture, society, art, technology, and more. He wrote books that were informative and insightful. He wrote books that were creative and captivating. He wrote books that were best-selling and award-winning.

He is most known for his book "How I wrote a million Wikipedia articles", where he shares his experience of being one of the most prolific contributors to the online encyclopedia. He reveals his methods, techniques, strategies, and secrets of writing high-quality articles on any subject in record time. He also discusses the benefits and challenges of being a Wikipedia editor in the age of information overload.

He is also known for his novel "Becoming the man", where he tells the story of a young man who goes through a series of transformations in his life. The novel explores themes such as identity, masculinity, self-discovery, love, loss, and redemption. The novel is based on his journey to becoming who he is today.

Copyright © 2024 Maher Asaad Baker

All rights reserved. No part of this document may be reproduced or transmitted in any form or by any means, electronic, mechanical, photocopying, recording, or otherwise, without prior written permission of the publisher.